JUDO FOR WOMEN

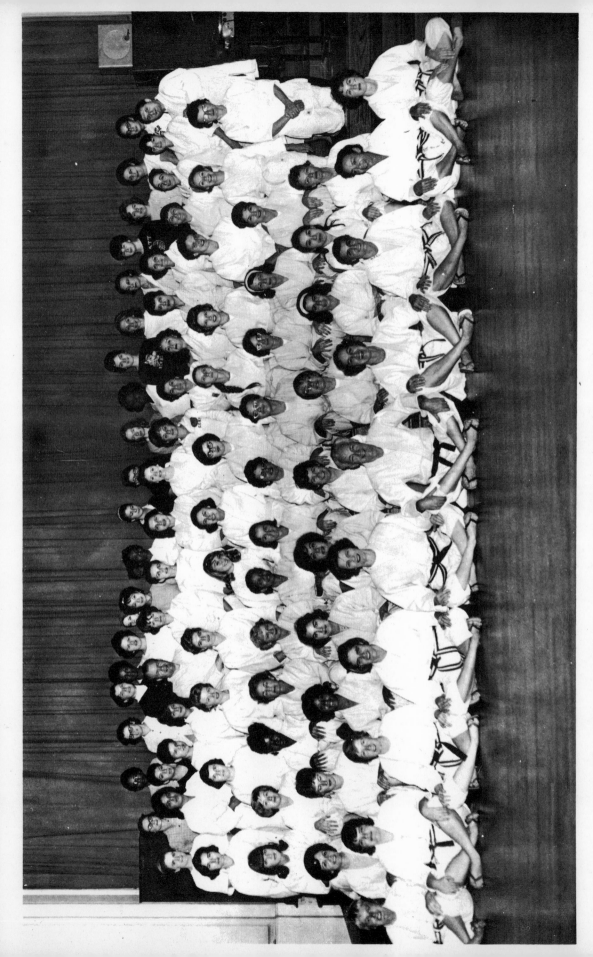

The author surrounded by her Friday night class at the Central Branch of the YWCA. New York

JUDO FOR WOMEN

A MANUAL OF SELF-DEFENSE

by RUTH HORAN

National Vice-Chairman, Women's Judo Committee of the United States; Women's Consultant, Metropolitan AAU Judo Committee; Life Member, Judo Black Belt Federation; Chief Instructor of the Central Branch YWCA Judo Group, New York; Women's Judo Instructor, St. John's University, New York.

Photographs by BERTIE McCOOL

CROWN PUBLISHERS, INC., NEW YORK

This book is dedicated with heartfelt gratitude
to my patient instructors, and my
wonderfully loyal students—but mainly to my husband
for his understanding and encouragement
and for being the "fall guy" in the photographs

CONTENTS

AUTHOR'S NOTE

This book is devoted to some of the basic self-defense techniques. It was started at the request of my students and was intended as a supplement to supervised instruction. No book could ever replace an instructor who can correct your mistakes when you make them. Keep in mind that for every attack there are many different ways to defend yourself. Nor can one book cover all attacks and defenses. This book will endeavor to teach you the principle involved in each move. By utilizing the basic principles you will be able to defend yourself against any attack.

R. H.

BRIEF HISTORY OF JUDO

Since the beginning of time, man has fought for existence. Among other things, he has fought against cold, fire, animals, and men. His fights with other men have taken many forms. The basic type, of course, is unarmed, or hand-to-hand, combat. The first man to realize that by seeming to give way he could draw his opponent into an off-balance position started the development of the method that, in Japan, eventually became known as Jujitsu, "The Gentle Art." It was known as the Gentle Art because its basic principle was to refrain from resisting strength with strength and instead to use an attacker's own aggressive motion, his own strength, against himself. The recorded history of Jujitsu in Japan goes back many centuries. But Jujitsu was not very gentle. It was taught as a combat method and, since it had no safety regulations, the accident rate must have been extremely high. Because of its violent nature, the students were generally of a criminal type; thus Jujitsu received a very bad name.

In the late 1870's, a young Japanese, Jigoro Kano, who was studying to be a teacher, became interested in the ancient Martial Arts of Old Japan. One of these arts was Jujitsu. This theory of gentleness appealed to Jigoro Kano, but he found in his studies of Jujitsu that unfortunately the general practice was a long way from its theory of gentleness. He continued to study with every Jujitsu Master he could find. He learned all of their secrets, and by comparing their methods, he worked out his own theory of Maximum Efficiency with Minimum Effort. With this principle as a guide, he reexamined the techniques of Jujitsu that he had learned. He rejected all moves not in keeping with this principle. He utilized the best of the Jujitsu techniques, eliminated the harmful ones, modified others, and added rules and regulations for safety in practice sessions. He refined and systematized these techniques and welded them into the ideal of World Benefit through Self-Perfection. He then added the second principle, that of Mutual Welfare and Benefit. He called his system of attack and defense Judo, which literally means "The Gentle Way."

In 1882 Professor Kano started his own school for Judo in an empty room of a Buddhist monastery. From this humble beginning grew the Kodokan Judo Institute in Tokyo. The Kodokan is at present the central organization for research and development and for the guidance of modern Judo throughout the world, and it grants degrees of rank. The Kodokan awards Dan Grade (Black Belt) upon the recommendation of the Black Belt Federations in other countries. All authentic Kodokan Dan Grade holders are registered with the Kodokan.

Professor Kano instituted a system for progression of study. Progress is rewarded by advancement in rank. The color of his belt denotes the rank of the Judo player.

Rank is divided into two classifications: Kyû grades and Dan grades. Kyû grades start with the sixth Kyû and work up to the first Kyû. Dan grades start with first Dan and progress upward. Thus, the beginner starts with sixth Kyû and continues as follows:

Rokkyû or Sixth Kyû	—White Belt
Gokyû or Fifth Kyû	—White Belt
Yonkyû Shikyû } or Fourth Kyû	—White Belt
Sankyû or Third Kyû	—Brown Belt
Nikyû or Second Kyû	—Brown Belt
Ikkyû or First Kyû	—Brown Belt
Shodan or First Dan	—Black Belt
Nidan or Second Dan	—Black Belt
Sandan or Third Dan	—Black Belt
Yodan or Fourth Dan	—Black Belt
Godan or Fifth Dan	—Black Belt
Rokudan or Sixth Dan	—Red and White or Black Belt
Shichidan or Seventh Dan	—Red and White or Black Belt
Hichidan or Eighth Dan	—Red and White or Black Belt
Kudan or Ninth Dan	—Red or Black Belt
Jûdan or Tenth Dan	—Red or Black Belt
Jûichidan or Eleventh Dan	—Red or Black Belt
Jûnidan or Twelfth Dan	—White (double width) or Black Belt
*Shidan or Doctor or Pastmaster	—White (double width) or Black Belt

The Tenth Dan is at present the highest rank ever awarded to a Judoka (Judo player) other than Professor Kano.

In America and Europe advancement may not be as rapid as at the Kodokan, owing to the limited time Americans and Europeans find for study.

In many clubs in these areas additional colors are used for the Kyû ranks, as follows:

Sixth Kyû	—White Belt
Fifth Kyû	—Yellow Belt
Fourth Kyû	—Green or Orange Belt
Third Kyû	—Green or Brown Belt
Second Kyû	—Brown or Blue Belt
First Kyû	—Brown Belt

A woman's belt has a white stripe running lengthwise down the center.

---

* Conferred only upon Professor Kano.

THE PHILOSOPHY AND AIMS

This book is intended to be a manual of basic self-defense moves for beginners. Therefore we will not attempt to explain the complete philosophy that is such an important part of the advanced study of Judo, although the Judo player must always keep in mind the founder's two basic principles, Maximum Efficiency with Minimum Effort and Mutual Welfare and Benefit. However, it is necessary to explain the responsibilities of a Judo student which are dictated by the philosophy. Judo is a contact sport, and injuries are always possible. I believe that with caution, courtesy, and strict observation of the safety rules, injuries can be kept to a minimum. In our classes we have had nothing more serious than a bump or bruise in over 40,000 student hours of lessons.

At all times you are responsible for the welfare of the person with whom you are working. You must never do anything to endanger him. You must never work incautiously or rashly.

Courtesy is an integral part of Judo. It is shown in the attitude of the Judoka (player) toward Judo, toward other players, and toward his instructors, all of whom must be treated with respect.

Judo is not a parlor trick and should not be used as such. There is a tendency for new Judo students to want to show off. Curb this tendency. Fooling around with these self-defense techniques can cause injuries. Approach your lessons with seriousness and diligence. Do not expect to learn any move by doing it only a few times. Only through repeated practice of each move can you master these techniques and do them instinctively.

Self-defense Judo techniques can save your life. Judo is a concealed weapon, but a weapon that, unlike a knife or gun, cannot be taken away and used against you.

Judo helps to quicken your reflexes. You may notice, as most of us have, that after a while you can anticipate an attack. Your "sixth sense" seems to warn you of evil intent. Avoid contact with your attacker if you can. The best use of Judo is never to have to use it at all. You will use Judo most efficiently by sensing trouble and avoiding it. There is an old saying in Judo that "Judo teaches you to run—but to run with confidence."

The ultimate aim of the study of Judo is to develop the student mentally, physically, and spiritually. While self-perfection should be your goal, such a goal is unobtainable. Yet your striving in that direction should never cease.

WHY JUDO FOR WOMEN?

Judo is perfectly suited to the needs and the temperament of women. Properly taught, it is truly the Gentle Way. The study of Judo strengthens character and at the same time develops a gentle personality, thus making a woman appear more feminine. You are taught methods designed to injure an attacker instantly. At the same time, you are responsible for the welfare of the person with whom you are practicing on the Judo mat. Therefore, you are on your honor not to misuse your knowledge. This, of course, develops your self-control. Most beginners have no intention of harming their partners. Yet by wanting to do their moves too quickly, before learning proper control, they can cause injuries. It is imperative to exercise self-control and to practice the moves slowly.

In learning to protect yourself you gain confidence in many ways. Enthusiastic interest in something outside yourself turns you into a more vital person, one who is interesting to others. This in turn helps you to feel more sure of yourself, and such self-confidence will make you more poised. Poise is merely the ability to meet any given situation with calmness and confidence.

The study of Judo also induces a true humility. Quite often the beginner in Judo feels stupid. This is because, while the basic moves appear quite simple, the coordination necessary to do them correctly can be achieved only after they have been practiced many times. As you progress in Judo you gain coordination, and learning the moves then becomes easier. But the more you know, the more you realize how little you know. This tends to deflate self-importance and to replace impatience with tolerance, arrogance with empathy, and false pride with humility. While you are striving for the unobtainable goal of perfection, there is no room for smug self-satisfaction. Each day is a new challenge to learn and improve.

If the only benefits derived from Judo were to our health, it would still be well worth the effort. The very nature of Judo captures the imagination. You become so fascinated with the Art, you think of nothing else while you are practicing. You forget your worries and cares. Judo serves to release tensions—mental as well as physical. You work off your frustrations. The physical activities of Judo give you a wonderful feeling of well-being.

One benefit of Judo is that it coordinates the entire body. Many activities and sports build or exercise only one set of muscles; Judo conditions all of them. It increases your flexibility, making you much more agile. This makes you feel and appear more graceful. By improving your circulation it improves your complexion. Because balance is so much a part of Judo, students generally note their posture improves. I have found with most of my students that the overweight reduce, the underweight gain. If the weight is right but its distribution is wrong, Judo can put the weight in the right places. Most of my students lose inches from their waist and hips in the first few months.

The overall benefits derived from studying Judo make the woman student appear and feel younger and more vibrant. The teen-age student appears more mature and womanly. She faces life with more confidence but without arrogance or egotism.

While nobody would claim that Judo has medical "cure-all" powers, I cannot overlook the physical and mental improvement in the condition of my students. One of my students, a woman with many problems in her private life, was having her yearly physical checkup. As the doctor was taking her blood pressure she started to tell him of her Judo classes. In her enthusiasm she talked for several minutes, during which he took her blood pressure several times. She naturally asked him why. He replied, "I don't know very much about Judo, but I strongly urge you to continue your studies. I was taking your blood pressure when you started telling me about your Judo classes. As you talked, your blood pressure went down fifty points. It's amazing." He went on to explain that tension had caused a temporary rise in her blood pressure. As she talked with enthusiasm of Judo, her cares were forgotten and the tension subsided.

I had two girls as students who were completely deaf. The inability to hear danger, such as automobiles and trucks—or potential attackers—was an important problem to them. They found that the study of Judo increased the speed of their reflexes and the so-called sixth sense. They could sense when someone approached. They became much more relaxed because they were freed from fear, fear of the unheard and unknown. Their headaches caused by tension disappeared.

To me one of the most important benefits of Judo is the feeling of fellowship. On the Judo mat artificial social distinctions disappear. We are all engaged in the same struggle. First, we learn to control and coordinate our own body, and then we learn how to control our partner's body and physical action. This creates a profound respect for the human body and consequently a much deeper respect for other people. As we advance in our studies, we learn to accept our partner as a true partner, not an opponent. This partnership is necessary to our progress. Thus, all true Judo players endeavor to help other Judo players to learn. When you are practicing Judo you will learn more quickly and enjoy it more if you trust the person with whom you are working. You must be relaxed. When you are thrown, the body must be relaxed in the proper position. Any muscle that is tight will transmit shock to the rest of the body. In trusting your partners with your body, you learn to trust them completely. This leads to a warm feeling of friendship and confidence in others.

Many people believe that Judo as a contact sport is only for the physically young and able. I firmly believe that Judo is of benefit to all ages and physical conditions and to both sexes. The science of Judo is based on the laws of nature. It is applied physics with emphasis on leverage and gravity. We endeavor in our training to learn to coordinate our bodies so that these principles work for us instead of against us. By using these principles, a small woman can keep under control a bigger, stronger opponent.

The oldest woman student I have ever taught was seventy-six. While she learned to defend herself well against an assailant, her greatest benefit from Judo was peace of mind. Age should not deter anyone from studying Judo. The teaching of Judo can and should be adapted to the needs and the abilities of the student. No two people ever learn at the same rate; yet the ultimate object remains the same for all. The instructor is responsible for teaching Judo techniques in the natural order. The moves must start with the easiest and progress to the more advanced. To teach an advanced technique before the student has learned the coordination necessary for the previous move is to invite injury to both student and partner. The instructor is responsible for actions and progress. No move should be taught until the instructor feels the student is ready for it.

It would be wonderful if husband, brother, or boyfriend were always with us to protect and defend us. Unfortunately there may be times when we are alone and unprotected. Avoiding trouble is the best use of Judo. But the knowledge that we can handle trouble if it is forced upon us does give a sense of security. A display of confidence will often make a would-be attacker think twice.

Here are a few cases in which Judo has played an important role in protecting several of my students.

It was the late afternoon of a bright fall day in New York. A woman instructor in a high-school printing class was hurrying along Forty-third Street and had almost reached Times Square. She became instinctively aware of a large man walking behind her. He suddenly appeared at her side and asked for a match. Saying she had no matches, she kept on walking. Without further ado, he seized her right wrist with both of his large hands. With a smile she quickly turned under his arms. Freeing her wrist from his grasp, she faced him with a broad grin. Her main thought was, "What will we do now?" He gaped. He stood and stared in utter amazement. His expression clearly said, "How could a five-foot-two-inch woman escape so easily from me, a six-foot-three-inch man?" He backed away in confusion. Thoroughly perplexed, he turned, ran for about ten feet, then stopped and looked again. With a look of utter disbelief, he took to his heels in earnest.

This one-hundred-and-ten-pound woman was one of my students in Judo. She had been studying for about a year at the time of the encounter. She said she smiled when he seized her because the move was so simple to escape from. She was pleased with herself because her escape had been a reflex action to his attack—just as it was supposed to be. She had spent a year practicing this type of escape, a year well spent if only for this moment. Her calmness, confidence, and disarming grin were effective weapons. What attacker wouldn't be knocked off balance to find his intended victim freeing herself so easily and then smiling at him?

If the attack had occurred in a deserted area, her reaction would have triggered a different counterattack. She would have incapacitated him while she still had the element of surprise working for her.

Another example concerns a young student nurse who was annoyed by a man walking next to her while she was hurrying through the subway crowds. He said, "Hello, baby. What's your hurry?" Ignoring him, she increased her speed. He would not be brushed off. Finally he grabbed her wrist and said, "Hey, babe, I said where are you going in such a hurry?" Snapping her wrist from his grasp, she replied, "I'm going to the YWCA to my Judo class!" When last seen he was beating a hasty retreat.

A tall middle-aged woman stepped from the subway train. As she walked down the platform, her heel caught in a grating, and the strap on her shoe broke. She walked slowly along, wondering how she could get home with her shoe in this condition. It had been such a pleasant day. In her attaché case was a bottle of expensive perfume she had saved for weeks to buy. By the time she approached the stairs to the street the other passengers had gone. Suddenly a man appeared at her side with a fistful of money. He said, "Look at the money I found. What should I do with it?" After a glance at him she said, "Turn it in to the station agent, I guess." She looked back at her shoe. In that instant he pushed her against the wall and held her there with his forearm. His other hand went to his trousers. Her first thought was of her perfume. Should she drop her attaché case and risk breaking the bottle? She thought, "No, so that eliminates wrist locks. I'll try pressure points. No, I'll just hit him with a Judo counterblow." With that, as she had been taught in Judo class, she raised her free hand to strike his neck with the side of the hand. He immediately released her and ran away. She was quite surprised. Almost two years before she had taken only eight lessons. How then had she remembered so many of the things she should do in such a circumstance, and why was she not in the least bit panicky? Mainly because she was angry. She went to the change booth attendant and told him of the attack. Busy counting change, he scarcely noticed her. Without looking up he advised her to "call a cop." Now she was really angry. As she started once again for the stairs at the end of the station, she heard a woman screaming. She thought, "Well, it worked once for me. Maybe I can help this woman." As she rounded a corner she could see the same man. The woman was prone on the platform. Looking up as my student came running toward him, he must have figured that two angry women were too much. This time he ran away for good.

A small high-school girl was balancing her books against the swaying of the subway car when she became aware of a man's body pressed against her back. As she had been taught in her Judo class, she moved away. He soon followed. She moved again. Again he followed. It was now obvious his moves were not accidental. She glanced over her shoulder before starting a countermeasure. She was surprised to see such a little man. Remembering the admonition that "the best use of Judo is to not have to use it at all," she reached into her purse for her wallet. The man did a double-take and moved away. She had shown him her Judo Rank Registration Card. Normally you do not let a potential attacker know that you know Judo. Why give away your secret weapon? In this case it was understandable. It may have made him think twice the next time. Perhaps another intended victim would not be so considerate.

These are just a few of the attacks and attempted attacks experienced by my students. Many others have had numerous occasions to use what they learned in their Judo classes to protect themselves. All have acquitted themselves well. Not one has suffered any harm at the hands of an attacker. I am very proud of all my students. I am also very grateful that when they needed to protect themselves, the Judo they had learned saved them from harm.

WHAT EVERY FEMALE STUDENT
OF JUDO SHOULD KNOW

The female body was not created to withstand as much physical force as the male body. Too much physical strain can be injurious. Before she is subjected to any hard, fast throws, the woman student must learn her falling techniques thoroughly. Some techniques must be adapted to her physical size and ability. Few women have had experience in contact sports prior to studying Judo. At first they may feel self-conscious about body contact, but as they become absorbed in their practice, they forget about themselves.

A woman beginner should wear comfortable clothing. A sweat shirt and loose-fitting slacks are appropriate. I also recommend a padded bra, one without wires. The student should buy a Judo suit, called a Judogi, as soon as possible. The Gi consists of a heavy jacket, trousers, and a belt. It is made to withstand a lot of use and cut so that the body has complete freedom to move without the suit binding. A woman must also wear a T-shirt under the jacket. The Judogi enables the student to take falls without getting mat burns. By using the Judogi, the thrower can control the person she is throwing so that the one being thrown will take a safe, comfortable fall.

Judo hygiene demands cleanliness of body and clothes. The Judogi must be clean and neat at all times. Fingernails and toenails should be short and clean. The use of a deodorant is recommended. If possible, the hair should be worn without pins or clips. Short hair or a ponytail is best. There must be no jewelry or pins worn on the Judo mat. There must be no chewing gum or anything else in the mouth while practicing. Good hygiene also dictates that the Judo player should empty the bowel and the bladder before practice. Refrain from eating heavily before practice.

Just as driving and liquor do not mix, so Judo and liquor do not mix, not so much for what you might do to yourself as for what you might do to your partner.

Most women students starting in Judo refrain from practice during the first day of the menstrual period. As she progresses in Judo and her physical condition improves through Judo exercises, the student finds that she needs refrain only from taking hard falls during this period. When she has been playing for several years she will probably find that she can enjoy normal Judo practice throughout the menstrual period. Each woman must find the most suitable practice schedule for her particular physical condition.

I have often been asked if the practice of Judo will increase sexual vitality. I feel that the study of Judo, in improving the physical condition, will naturally increase the vitality of all bodily functions. Several of my students who were

9

childless though married for five years or more became pregnant within a year of starting Judo. These women continued to practice a modified form of Judo until about the fifth month. They did the Judo exercises throughout their pregnancy, picking up full practice sessions again soon after the birth. They not only felt fine throughout their pregnancy, but regained their figures after the birth. Naturally they were under a doctor's care and were following his directions.

In our classes at the YWCA in New York and New Jersey, the first eight weeks are devoted to self-defense. This serves two purposes. First, students learn the rudiments of defending themselves while they are learning to co-ordinate their bodies. Second, they gain an understanding of what Judo is meant to be. During this period they are not thrown. Thus, many women who do not wish to be thrown still learn to defend themselves. After they come to understand what Judo means the majority of them usually decide to stay in Judo and to learn to fall and to throw. The second eight-week period is spent learning the rudiments of falling and the first simple throws, plus more advanced self-defense techniques. At the end of this second eight-week period, when the student has gained proficiency and improved her coordination, she progresses to the advanced classes. In the advanced classes she starts a general study of Judo techniques as well as continuing the study of self-defense. She stays in the advanced class as long as she stays in Judo.

Professor Kano set up a course of instruction of the forty basic moves. This is called the Gokyo. The Gokyo is five sets of eight techniques each, starting with the simplest and progressing to the more difficult.

Women in Judo earn promotion in rank by gaining proficiency in technique in the moves of the Gokyo and by demonstrating knowledge and technical ability in the Formal Katas, exercises in which the basic moves are performed in a set order. Promotion in rank is given to players with good moral character, a mature Judo attitude, and a knowledge of Judo philosophy and technique. Men can progress in rank in Judo by proficiency in contest. Women do not compete in contests, but they are expected to have some proficiency in Randori (practice of technique in free play). For grading purposes they are tested on their knowledge and technique. This also includes knowledge of Katame waza, or mat technique; Shime waza, or Judo choking technique; and Kansetsu waza, or locking technique.

Now, if I may, a few words to the serious Judo student. When I first saw a Judo demonstration I was fascinated and intrigued. I found a Judo class at a local YWCA and started studying Judo soon after. I was fortunate in that the instructor was so well suited to my needs and temperament. He taught his students to love and respect Judo with the same dedication he felt. With a good instructor you will, naturally, progress more rapidly. I feel most women enjoy learning Judo more and learn it better from a competent woman teacher in a women's Judo class. There are, unfortunately, not enough of these available. Generally speaking, the best procedure is to study with the highest-ranking instructor available. But the instructor and student must be compatible. You may learn more from a lower-ranking instructor if his methods better fit your abilities and temperament.

Be loyal to your club, to your instructor, and to your Judo teammates. In their eagerness to practice Judo, some students play in clubs other than their own. This should only be done with the prior knowledge and approval of your instructor. Be loyal to Judo. Remember if others have no knowledge of Judo but know that you are a Judo student, they may judge all Judo by your words and actions. Earn their respect and they will respect Judo. Show your regard for Judo in thought, word, and deed and Judo will enrich your life. Be proud of Judo and Judo will be proud of you.

Try to attend your Judo classes regularly. Right from the start, set certain nights apart for Judo and, unless an emergency intervenes, make it a habit to be there. We all have days when we are tired and do not really feel like physical activity. Go to Judo anyway. You will feel physically better after class. Practice technique. In Judo you will have days when nothing you do is as good as you know you are capable of doing. Keep practicing. Success in anything is only the power of continual effort. When we are faced with failure, a little more persistence and effort often brings success. The only failure is in no longer trying. The only defeat is in accepting failure. Give the best that is in you to whatever you do and you are bound to succeed.

I have dedicated my life to the study of Judo and have endeavored to foster a better understanding of what the art of Judo really means. Jim Gordon, the noted sports announcer, once said in a radio interview that I was a "missionary for Judo." I only know that I feel that the study of Judo in teaching the control of your body and your emotions leads to a better understanding of others and of life. Mutual understanding is needed by all humanity. One of my students had suffered a particularly trying experience before she started Judo. She later told me she felt that Judo had literally taught her to live again. She had lost all faith in people but through Judo she learned to understand herself better. She built a new life based on trust and understanding.

A WORD OF CAUTION

There are several points that should be explained before we start. Primarily you must understand that you will not become a Judo expert by practicing a few escapes. You will learn how to defend yourself against the most common attacks, but how proficient you become depends entirely upon how well you practice. The moves in this book start with the simplest forms and gradually progress to the more difficult ones. If you diligently practice the basic forms until you have perfected them, you will develop the coordination necessary for the more advanced forms. It is somewhat similar to learning a foreign language. You would not expect to converse fluently after taking a few lessons. It all depends upon how much you practice. Do not skip to the advanced moves until you can do each preceding move easily. Do not try for speed. Do each move slowly, with rhythm, and speed will come naturally.

Learn to maintain your balance at all times. Generally speaking, this is best achieved by keeping the weight on the balls of both feet with the knees slightly bent. In most cases, balance will be better if the torso remains upright, without bending at the waist. Most of the bending should be done at the knees.

All moves must be done slowly and cautiously. When applying locks and chokes, it is particularly important that the pressure be consistent. Never apply them with a jerky motion. The sign of submission in Judo is generally two rapid slaps on yourself, on the mat, or on your opponent. When this sign is given, the hold must be released immediately.

Your progress will be more rapid if you have a partner who approaches this study in a helpful manner. You must help each other to learn. In the beginning, do not try to prove that the moves work; just go through the motions until you develop coordination and rhythm. When the move is well coordinated, it will work against anyone.

BASIC EXERCISES

Before you start Judo practice you must learn the basic exercises. These are intended to make your body more flexible. It is therefore important that you stay as relaxed as possible. The more relaxed you are when exercising, the greater the flexibility you will achieve. Do not attempt to do too much at the start. On each move, go only as far as your body can easily manage. You will find that each time you repeat the exercises, your body becomes a little more flexible and you can bend a little farther. Keep your knees relaxed. Before starting your Judo practice, you must always exercise. This will condition your body so that proficiency in the Judo techniques will develop more easily. Also, warming-up exercises reduce the chances of your suffering stiff muscles from Judo practice.

EXERCISE 1

2. Turn the upper part of your body to the left as far as it will comfortably go.

1. Raise your arms from your sides until they extend straight out from the shoulders, parallel to the ground. Let the hands hang loosely, like a scarecrow's. Your feet should be planted about shoulder-width apart; knees relaxed.

3. Turn back to the right. Let the arms swing loosely at shoulder height.

4. Repeat 10 times. This works wonders for your waist and loosens the entire torso.

EXERCISE 2

1. Arms extended to each side at shoulder height as in Exercise 1. Feet shoulder-width apart; knees slightly bent.

2. Reaching over your head with your left hand, bend your waist to the right. Bring your hand as close to the floor as is easily possible. Do not force it. Try 4 times with the left hand and then stand upright, arms extended at sides.

3. Now raise your right hand and bend to the left 4 times.

4. Do the complete exercise twice. This loosens the entire body—arms, legs, and torso.

EXERCISE 3

1. Feet apart, extend your arms and hands straight out in front of you, palms down, fingers spread.

2. Clench your fists; stretch your fingers.

3. Repeat 10 times. This loosens fingers, hands, and wrists.

EXERCISE 4

1. Feet apart, extend your arms straight out in front of you.

2. Make fists, palms down.

3. Keeping your elbows at shoulder level and your wrists straight, pull your fists in to your chest.

4. Repeat 10 times. This loosens arms and shoulders. It has a side benefit of developing the breast area.

EXERCISE 5

1. Let your head hang loosely forward, as relaxed as possible.

2. Gently roll your head around in a circle, to the right, back, to the left, and forward. Repeat.

3. Roll the head around in the opposite direction. Repeat.

4. This is intended to loosen the neck. Keep your neck as relaxed as possible. If the neck muscles are tight, you might feel dizzy. Loosen up.

EXERCISE 6

1. Feet about shoulder-width apart. Hands on hips.

2. Pivot on the balls of the feet to the right through an angle of 90 degrees. Shift weight forward onto your right foot, bending your right knee. Keep your left leg straight but not rigid, your left foot flat on the floor.

3. Bend your right knee farther; then shift your weight back to your left foot, straightening your right leg. Repeat 4 times.

4. Pivot 180 degrees to your left, bending your left knee. Repeat the same exercise to the left 4 times.

5. Do the complete exercise twice. This loosens the ligaments and muscles in the front of the thighs and the hip area.

EXERCISE 7

1. Repeat the movements of Exercise 6, but taking a wider stance, carrying your weight farther forward, and until you are almost squatting on your heel.

2. Do the complete exercise twice.

EXERCISE 8

1. At the end of Exercise 7, shift your weight forward again onto your left foot. Retaining the position of your legs, turn on the ball of your left foot to face front. With your right leg extended straight out to your right and with the toes of your right foot raised and your right heel on the mat, work the ligaments and muscles in the back of your right leg by bouncing the body up and down on the left heel.

2. Draw your right foot up under you, extend your left leg, and work on the left leg in the same way.

19

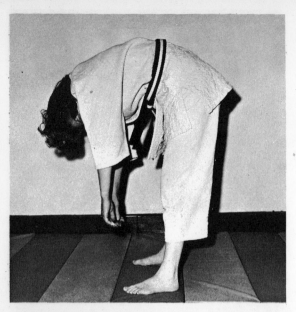

EXERCISE 9

1. Feet shoulder-width apart, knees relaxed.

2. Bend forward and let your arms hang relaxed in front of you. Keep the entire body as relaxed as a rag doll.

3. Gently let the body bob up and down.

4. This loosens back and legs.

EXERCISE 10

1. With your hands clasped behind your head, bend forward as low as possible. Exerting no pressure with hands, push head toward knees 4 times.

2. Straighten up, place your hands on your hips and lean back as far as possible. When you lean back, shift your hips forward and your weight will shift to the balls of your feet. Push hips forward and upper body back 4 times.

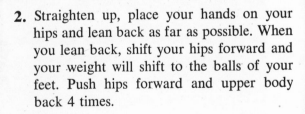

3. Do entire exercise twice. Loosens back and legs.

EXERCISE 11

1. Feet shoulder-width apart; knees relaxed.

2. With hands clasped behind head, elbows high, bend forward and touch your right elbow to your left knee. Stand up.

3. Repeat movement, touching left elbow to right knee.

4. Repeat exercise 10 times. Loosens back and legs.

EXERCISE 12

1. Sit on the floor, legs extended, feet wide apart, knees relaxed.

2. Extend your arms in front of you close together.

3. Keeping arms in front of you, bend forward 4 times as though to touch your head to your left knee. Straighten up.

4. Bend forward 4 times as though to touch your head to the floor between your knees. Straighten up.

5. Bend forward 4 times as though to touch your head to your right knee. Straighten up.

6. Repeat complete exercise 4 times.

7. Loosens entire body.

ISOMETRIC EXERCISES

The Judo exercises in Exercises 1 through 12 are designed to limber up the body and make it more agile and flexible. Isometric exercises are intended to increase the strength and fitness of individual muscles or groups of muscles. In each exercise you tense a muscle and hold it as tense as possible for six seconds. Isometric exercises can be performed at almost any time without special clothing or apparatus. Women not wanting to develop bulging muscles will find isometric exercise the perfect way to achieve muscle tone without a muscular appearance. Isometrics could be called "do-it-yourself instant fitness." Actually they do not produce instant fitness but they are a repetition of a series of exercises that take up little more than one minute each day. Surely everyone can spare one minute a day to look better and feel better?

Remember now, in each position given, you must exert the maximum amount of force possible and hold that position for six seconds (count from 1001 to 1006). Breathe normally; do not hold your breath.

As the first four exercises are done in a lying position, they can be performed before you get out of bed in the morning. I have found they help me to wake up quicker and, I might add, in a more cheerful attitude of mind. Exercises 13 and 14 can be done in either order, depending upon your position when you wake up. Keep in mind that it is the holding action that will do the work for you, so hold each pose as hard as you can.

ISOMETRIC EXERCISE 1

1. In a prone position on your stomach, extend your arms from the shoulder. If you are in a narrow bed, place your hands as far apart as possible.
2. Push your palms down on the bed as though you are trying to clap your hands in front of you. Do not allow your body to rise from the bed. Hold for 6 seconds. This tones the chest muscles. Good chest-muscle tone supports and lifts the breasts.

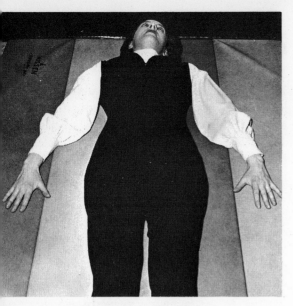

ISOMETRIC EXERCISE 2

1. Lie in a supine position on your back with your arms at your sides, palms down.

2. Grip the bed as though you are trying to make a fist right through the mattress and push your arms back. Hold for 6 seconds. This tones the chest, fingers, and arms with particular action of the back of the upper arms.

ISOMETRIC EXERCISE 3

1. Lying on your back, cross your ankles and lock your feet together.

2. Try to pull your legs apart. Hold for 6 seconds. This works on two sets of leg and thigh muscles, the ones that are attempting to separate your legs as well as the ankle and foot muscles that hold them together.

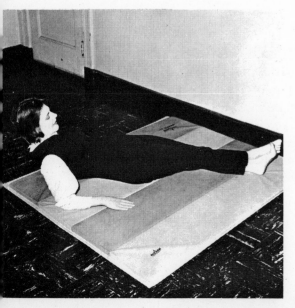

ISOMETRIC EXERCISE 4

1. Lying on your back, cross your ankles and lock your feet together. Support the upper part of your body on your elbows and forearms.

2. Tense your leg muscles and your buttocks and raise hips.

3. This action lifts your body so that you are resting on your forearms and heels. Hold for 6 seconds. This tones legs, buttocks, and chest and shoulder muscles.

ISOMETRIC EXERCISE 5

1. Stand in a doorway.
2. Place your hands, palm out, just above head height against the sides of the door frame.
3. Push as hard as you can for 6 seconds. Tones chest, shoulder, and arm muscles. Good for lifting and developing the breast line.

ISOMETRIC EXERCISE 6

1. Stand in a doorway.
2. Place the back of the hands against the sides of the door frame.
3. Push hard for 6 seconds. Tones the back of the upper arms.

ISOMETRIC EXERCISE 7

1. Stand with your back against the door jamb.
2. Lift the chest and pull the stomach in as far as you can. Hold for 6 seconds. This exercise practiced daily will give you that nice flat tummy you would like. It can be practiced almost anywhere, sitting or standing.

ISOMETRIC EXERCISE 8

1. Stand in a doorway with your back to the door jamb.
2. Lift one foot at a time and push the sole against the door jamb behind you. Hold for 6 seconds. This tones hips, buttocks, and leg muscles.

ISOMETRIC EXERCISE 9

1. Stand in a doorway facing the door jamb.
2. Place the hands on either side of the wall in which the door is set and push them toward each other. Hold for 6 seconds. This tones chest, shoulder, and arm muscles.

ISOMETRIC EXERCISE 10

1. Stand facing the wall.
2. Place hands shoulder-high against the wall and push. Hold for 6 seconds. Tones back, shoulders, and arms.

ISOMETRIC EXERCISE 11

1. Turn your head far to the left and stick out your lower lip and jaw. Hold for 6 seconds.
2. Turn your head to the front and repeat.
3. Turn your head to the right and repeat. Works wonders on chin and neck muscles.

 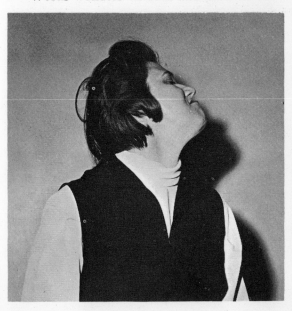

UKEMI — THE ART OF FALLING

Ukemi is the Judo method of breakfall. This system teaches safe and easy falls. When you fall to the mat or are thrown you must either break your fall with a slap or dissipate the force of the fall with a rolling motion of your body. The slap on the mat acts as a shock absorber and enables the body to land safely. You must practice only on a mat. Do not practice falls or slapping exercises on the bare floor or rug. It is desirable for the student to learn Ukemi and falling methods under an instructor's supervision, if at all possible. This section should therefore be considered a supplement to that instruction.

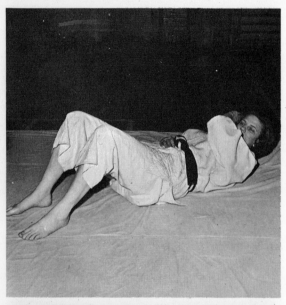

SLAPPING EXERCISE 1 —SINGLE SLAP

1. Lie flat on your back on the mat, knees raised, feet flat on the mat about 8 inches apart.

2. Place your right hand on your belt. Raise your left hand close to your right ear, elbow bent, palm forward. This is the slapping position for the hand.

3. Bring the arm down to your left side at an angle of approximately 30 degrees to your body, fingers together and relaxed.

4. Your elbow and wrist must be straight when your hand reaches the mat. The motion should be as though you are swatting a mosquito with your left hand. Your hand must move directly from your ear to the mat. Use shoulder and back muscles rather than forearm muscles for slapping. Stay relaxed; do not tighten arm muscles.

5. The hand should bounce off the mat and return to your ear. This should happen naturally; do not force the return.

6. Start slowly, then increase speed and power.

7. Repeat 10 times with each hand.

SLAPPING EXERCISE 2
—DOUBLE SLAP

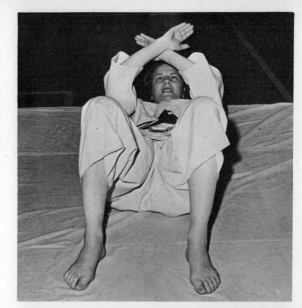

1. Lie flat on your back, knees raised, feet flat on the mat about 8 inches apart.
2. Raise both arms, elbows bent, fingers together, palms facing up. Cross your wrists about 8 inches in front of your eyes. This is the two-handed slapping position.

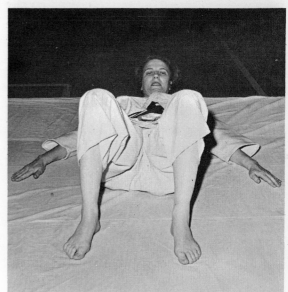

3. Slap the mat with both hands simultaneously, bringing the arms down straight and at an angle of approximately 30 degrees to the side of the body.
4. The hands must bounce off the mat and return to their starting position with a whipping motion.
5. Repeat 10 times.

SLAPPING EXERCISE 3
—BACKWARD ROLL

1. Assume a sitting position with knees raised, feet slightly apart, arms raised in the slapping position.
2. Hunch your shoulders forward close to your knees. Keep your back rounded. Rest forearms on knees.
3. Put your chin on your chest and leave it there.

4. Roll back like a ball until your head touches the floor and your body curls up above it. Return to sitting position. Keep round. Stay relaxed.

5. Practice 5 times.

SLAPPING EXERCISE 4
—BACKWARD ROLL WITH
DOUBLE SLAP

1. Do Slapping Exercise 3, adding the double slap described in Slapping Exercise 2.

2. Start your slap as you start your rolling motion. Your hands should slap the mat at approximately the same time that your shoulders reach the mat.

3. Practice 5 times.

SLAPPING EXERCISE 5 —BACKWARD ROLL SLAP FROM SQUATTING POSITION

1. Rest on ball of your left foot, your right foot flat and slightly advanced. Hunch the back so that the shoulders approach the knees. Keep chin on chest. Raise your arms in slapping position.

2. Roll straight back, keeping your left heel in contact with your body. Simply roll down onto your left foot. This rolls your body onto the mat. Do not drop your body or throw it backward.

3. Keep round and relaxed and let your momentum roll your legs up above your head.

4. Slap the mat with both hands, arms straight and at an angle of 30 degrees to the side of the body. The slap motion should start as you start to roll back. It should be synchronized with your rolling motion.

5. Your hands should reach the mat just as your shoulders reach the mat.

6. Practice 5 times.

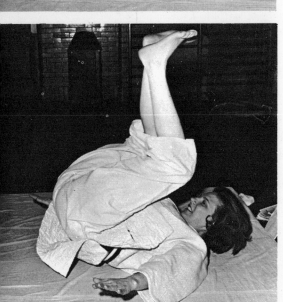

SLAPPING EXERCISE 6
—SIDE POSITION SLAP

1. Lie on your left side with your left knee bent. The outside of your left leg lies flat on the mat, the sole of the left foot at right angles to the mat. Your left thigh forms an angle of approximately 45 degrees with an imaginary line down the center of your body. Your right shoulder is off the mat. The sole of the left foot is close to the inside of your right foot. The right foot is flat on the mat.

2. Place your right hand on your belt. Raise the left hand close to your right ear in slapping position. Slap the hand down on the mat so that your left arm lies parallel to your left thigh. Stay relaxed.

3. Repeat the exercise on your right side.

4. Practice 10 times.

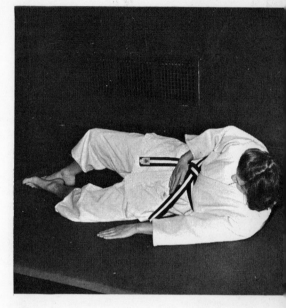

SLAPPING EXERCISE 7
—SIDE FALL SLAP I

1. Assume a sitting position with knees raised and back rounded.

2. Raise left hand to slap position, right forearm resting on right knee.

3. Drop chin on chest. Dropping the left leg sideways onto the mat and keeping the right foot flat, roll obliquely to the left and back onto your left side into the position described in Slapping Exercise 6, slapping the left hand on the mat. Stay relaxed.

4. Start your slap as you start to roll. Bounce slap.

5. Practice 5 times on each side.

SLAPPING EXERCISE 8 —SIDE FALL SLAP II

1. Assume a sitting position. Raise the right knee; extend the left leg so that it points obliquely across the body slightly to right of front. The outside of the left foot and ankle are in contact with the mat, left knee bent. Right hand on right knee.

2. Raise your left hand to slap position.

3. Roll obliquely to the left and back onto your left side as in Slapping Exercises 6 and 7, slapping the mat with your left hand. In this exercise the body must be round and must roll. Keep your back curved and your shoulders slightly hunched. Stay relaxed.

4. Maintain the curve of your body so that when your slap reaches the mat the rolling motion will lift your feet and legs from the mat.

5. Practice 5 times on each side.

SLAPPING EXERCISE 9
—SIDE FALL SLAP
SQUATTING POSITION

The beginner may find this move easier to coordinate if she has a partner. Squat in front of your partner at right angles to her body. Grasp the front of her clothing with your right hand. It is suggested that she wear a Judogi or heavy sweatshirt. The partner will hold your right sleeve above the elbow with both hands. She will support you as you roll.

1. Sit on your right heel in a squatting position, weight on your right foot. In the preliminary side falls, you may place your right hand on the mat for balance. After you have developed coordination and balance in this move, the hand that is not slapping should be held at your belt.

2. Raise your left hand to your right ear in the slap position.

3. Slide your left foot forward and slightly to the right, outside edge of left foot in contact with mat. Roll obliquely back and to the left as in Slapping Exercise 8, slapping the left hand on the mat. Stay relaxed.

4. Keep the body round and roll as in Slapping Exercise 8.

5. Start your slap as you start your roll. Slap as the shoulders reach mat. Bounce hand in slap.

6. Practice 5 times on each side, first with partner then alone.

SLAPPING EXERCISE 10
—SIDE FALL SLAP
STANDING POSITION

1. As in Slapping Exercise 9, start with a partner then continue alone. Stand at right angles to your partner. Stand with right hand on your belt or partner's lapel.

2. Step obliquely forward and to the right with your right foot.

3. Slide your left foot diagonally across in front of your right foot as you sink onto your right heel in a squatting position.

4. Roll obliquely back and to your left as in Slapping Exercise 9 and slap with your left hand. Roll legs up.

5. Practice 5 times each side.

JUDO TECHNIQUES

1. BASIC HAND ESCAPE

attack:

Your partner faces you and grips your right wrist with his left hand in a normal manner, i.e., thumb on the inside of your wrist pointing down, arms relaxed. Have your partner hold firmly but not too tightly in the beginning, so as to learn to coordinate the movements first. Once your body learns to assume the correct position the actual escape will be easy. Your partner should hold with his hands but his arms should be bent and relaxed. The straighter his arms, the more you must bend your knees and the lower you must go.

escape:

1. Step in between your partner's feet with your right foot, bend your right knee, and shift your weight onto your right foot as you drive your right elbow forward in a semicircular motion *under* your partner's hand.

2. Use his grip as the center of the circle described by your elbow. Do not allow your elbow to rise up sideways. Keep balanced, use leverage, and aim your elbow toward his solar plexus. Regardless of his strength, height, or weight, you can escape from his grip easily because you are using the strength of your entire body against the muscle in the last joint of his thumb.

practice:

To develop the correct arm motion, stand relaxed. Bend your right arm at the elbow so that the forearm is at right angles with the upper arm. Make a fist and gently swing your elbow in a circular motion until your fist passes close to your right ear. Make sure that the elbow stays bent at approximately a right angle. This ensures that you will be moving your arm by using your shoulder and back muscles rather than the muscles in your forearm. You will need very little strength. The gentle swing combined with the correct body position in relation to your opponent will ensure your escape. You must always make a fist when doing hand escapes. This keeps your wrist straight and strong.

2. CROSS-HAND ESCAPE

attack:

Your partner grips your left wrist with his left hand in the usual manner, i.e., thumb on the outside of your wrist pointing down, arms relaxed.

escape:

The escape is the same motion as in the Basic Hand Escape. Be certain that you step in straight toward the center of your partner's body and aim your elbow directly at his solar plexus.

3. BASIC TWO-HAND ESCAPE

attack:

Your attacker grips both of your wrists in the usual way, i.e., his thumbs on the inside of your wrists pointing down, arms relaxed.

escape:

Since he is gripping both of your wrists, you may step in with either foot as in the previous hand escapes. The escape motion is the same as in the single hand escapes. Both of your elbows must travel in a circular motion under his hands. Aim both of your elbows at his mid-section.

4. BASIC FRONT CHOKE ESCAPE

attack:

Your partner chokes you with his hands from the front. His arms are straight.

escape:

1. Raise your arm straight up, close to your right ear. At the first practices, to ensure that your arm is close to your head, reach over your head and touch your left ear with your fingers.

2. Take a small step back with your left foot and pivot on both feet to your left. Keep your shoulders level as you turn and your torso straight. Do not bend sideways at the waist. Push your right shoulder forward toward his left wrist.

3. As you continue to pivot, your shoulder will force his hand off your neck. If he is holding very tightly the motion will lock his left wrist between your right shoulder and your neck. If his grip is rigid and the wrist will not bend, the action will break his wrist. This is true of most of these techniques: the greater the force the attacker uses against you, the more vulnerable he becomes.

4. It is important in this move that your arm be held tightly against your ear *before* you start to turn. If you turn with the arm only partway up, you will be using only arm strength against his arm. We presume a real attacker will be stronger than you. If he isn't, you could probably handle him without Judo. Judo makes it easier.

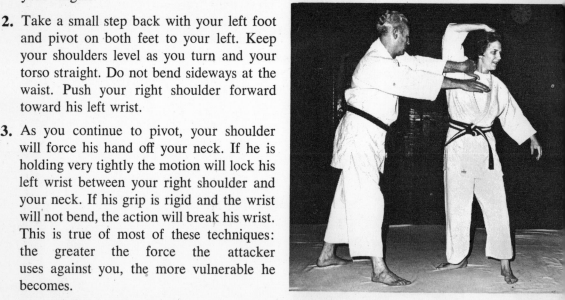

practice:

Practice this move very slowly so that you wil not hurt your partner's wrist. I suggest that yo practice the pivot alone to see how your balanc can best be maintained as you turn. Practic with either arm raised, always turning towar the attacker's wrist.

5. BASIC REAR CHOKE ESCAPE

attack:

Your partner chokes you with his bare hands from the rear with his arms straight.

escape:

1. Raise your right arm above and close to your head as you did in the preceding move.

2. Pivot on your left foot and step back and around your partner's left foot with your right foot.

3. This will leave you face to face with your partner. Always turn your raised arm toward your partner's wrist. In the Rear Choke Escape the raised right arm turns back toward his right wrist.

practice:

Practice raising each arm so that you become proficient in the move, whichever side you use.

Before you proceed any further, practice the three hand escapes and the two choke escapes until your body moves smoothly with coordination. Pay particular attention to your balance; it must be maintained at all times.

43

COUNTERATTACKS, OR ATEWAZA
— THE ART OF ATTACKING
THE VITAL POINTS OF THE BODY

6. COUNTERATTACKS FOR BASIC ESCAPES

This section starts with counterattacks that can be used in conjunction with the basic escapes just learned. The basic escapes can be used alone to free yourself from your assailant's grip. If you anticipate that your attacker intends to harm you, then you must counterattack immediately while you still have the element of surprise on your side. Your counterattack must be a natural follow-through from whichever escape technique has been used. It is important to maintain your balance at all times so that you will be in a position to strike if you must. The counterattack to use will be determined by your position in relation to your attacker. Always use the strength of your body, not that of your arm alone. The body should pivot on the balls of the feet. The knees should be slightly bent. The arm should whip the blow and the hand should strike with a bouncing motion. This concentrates the full power of the blow into one split second of force.

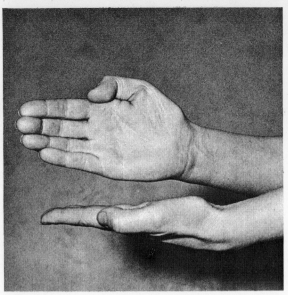

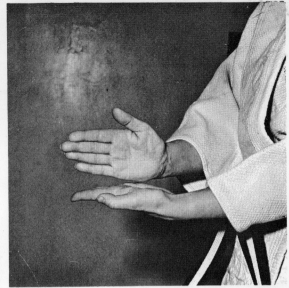

practice:

1. Hold your right hand straight, fingers together. Bounce the outer edge of this hand against the palm of your other hand. In counterattacks following basic escapes you strike with the edge of the hand midway between the wrist and the little-finger knuckle.

2. Now bring your forearm up parallel with your shoulders, elbow bent. Pivot the body, knees bent, to the left if you are using your right hand, to the right if you are using your left hand. Pivot back again and strike at an imaginary target in front of you. Whip the arm out and bounce the blow where your imaginary target is standing. *Do not strike at your partner*. Strike at a point several inches away from the actual target point.

45

3. Now practice again the Basic Hand Escape and the Cross-Hand Escape that you learned in the previous chapter. After you have escaped, continue the upward movement of your arm to gain a greater amount of power and bring the hand down to strike against your partner's collarbone. The collarbone is very vulnerable because of its location. It will break under a pressure of approximately 15 pounds. Maintain your balance. Strike with a whipping motion against either side of the collarbone. Your position in relation to your partner will determine which side to strike. Remember your blow must be a natural follow-through from your position at the end of the escape. Use your own momentum. *Do not strike your partner.*

4. Practice again the Basic Two-Hand Escape described in the previous chapter. After you have broken your attacker's hold, continue the upward movement of the arms and bring them down to strike with the outer edges of both hands against your attacker's collarbone. Remember to keep well balanced and to strike with a bouncing motion. *Do not strike your partner.*

Make your hand bounce about 6 inches from your partner. *Do not actually touch your partner in practice.* At the same time bring your other hand up to protect your face. In practice your partner should bring his hand up close to his neck after you escape so that if you misjudge the distance you will hit his hand rather than his neck.

5. Practice again the basic Front Choke Escape learned in the previous chapter. After you have turned and your partner's hand slips from your neck, continue your turn through about another 20 degrees and bring your right forearm parallel with your shoulder, elbow bent. Pivot back toward your partner and strike at the side of your attacker's neck. A blow in this area momentarily blocks the flow of blood to the brain, knocking your adversary unconscious. If your attacker is much taller than you are, you may not be able to reach up to his neck. In this case, your counterblow will be directed at the lower rib cage. A blow here can collapse a lung and cause unconsciousness.

6. Practice again the Basic Rear Choke Escape. Keep your right arm raised until your attacker's right hand has slipped from your neck. Continue your turn, bringing your right forearm down parallel with your shoulders and making a fist with your right hand. Place the fist in the palm of your left hand and clasp it with the fingers. Both your elbows should be bent. Keep both wrists as straight as possible. When you have reached the fully wound-up position, pivot back, striking at the left side of your attacker's jaw with the forward part of your right elbow. This is the Forward Elbow Smash. *Do not hit your partner.*

practice:

Stand alone with your arms raised shoulder-high, fists clasped as explained above, and practice striking at an imaginary target. Keep balanced with your knees slightly bent. Pivot on the balls of both feet and bounce the blow. This is the Elbow Smash position. Practice striking with the forward part of the elbow as it is used in the Basic Rear Choke Escape Counterattack. Practice striking with each elbow. Then practice pivoting from side to side and striking with the back part of the elbow at the ribs of an attacker standing behind you. This will be used in some of the later counterattacks. Practice escaping from the Rear Choke and countering with each arm.

7. PRESSURE POINTS

Keep in mind that Judo should not be used aggressively against an innocent person. It is most effective when used as a defensive weapon against an attacker. If someone is attacking you, it is obvious that you must defend yourself. If he is merely being annoying, it will be in your best interest to walk away or to ignore him. If someone attempts to embrace you and refuses to release you when asked, you can use pressure on his nerve centers to effect your release. Action against pressure points (nerve centers) should be taken only against an annoying, rather than a dangerous, attack.

I am sure you have at some time hit your elbow on the "funny bone." This is a pressure point, or nerve center. Most people experience a sharp sensation, almost like an electric shock, when this happens. If the blow is hard enough, you may feel as though the hand has fallen asleep. This is a temporary paralysis caused by the pressure on the nerve center. There are some who do not feel this sharp sensation, but the paralysis is just as effective in their case, although perhaps not as quick. For example, you may have had your foot "go to sleep" while sitting. But often you are not aware of it until you stand up. This is the paralysis caused by pressure on a nerve. There was no sharp pain, only the paralysis.

There are nerve centers, or pressure points, at every joint in the body. Some are more accessible than others. As a beginner you will be taught a few of the basic points. If you continue in Judo your instructor will teach you the more advanced (and dangerous) points, but only when you have the judgment to use them wisely.

The correct position of your fingers is important. Make a circle with your thumb and index finger. The inside of the tip of the thumb should be touching the inside of the tip of the index finger. Try to keep the opening as round as possible. The other three fingers should be held close to the index finger, supporting it. The motion is a pinching one, but the pads of the thumb and fingers do not touch, only the sides of the tips. By using the edges of the thumb and index finger, the pressure is concentrated in a small contact area and thus increased in force. If you use the pads, the force is dissipated over a larger area and is not as effective.

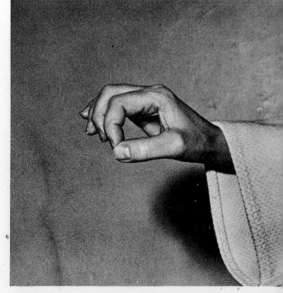

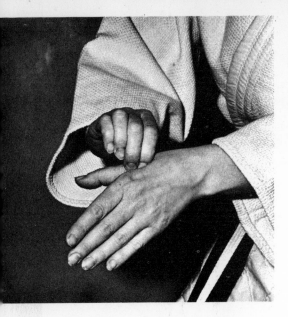

practice:

1. Hold your left hand in front of you and feel the bone running down the back of the hand from the index finger. It meets the bone from the thumb close to the base of the hand. Place the side of the tip of your right index finger just in front of this joint. Place the side of the tip of your right thumb under your left thumb—around the muscle—and pinch. This will help you to learn the correct pinching position.

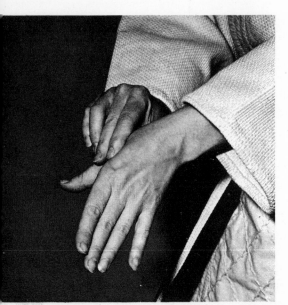

2. Try it once using the pads of the fingers instead of the tips and notice how much less effective it is.

FRONT PIN

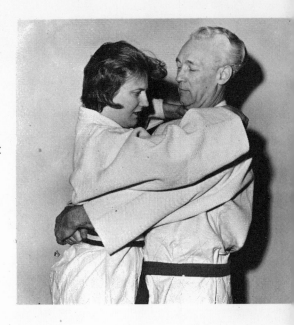

attack:

Your partner embraces you from the front in an annoying (not a dangerous) manner.

escape:

Try to talk your way out of his grip. Make it clear you are displeased. If he persists in holding you, use pressure points to free yourself. Place the tips of your thumbs, pointing down, against the top of his collarbone, one on each side, close to the neck at a point in the center of the triangle formed by the neck, the collar bone, and the muscle on the top of the shoulder. The knuckles of the thumbs are bent. Curl your fingers over his shoulders in the correct position and apply pressure with a pinching motion. Be sure to use the sides of the thumbs and the sides of the index fingers. Support your index fingers with your other fingers. Use a sharp, quick motion and move away from your molester as soon as you feel his grip loosen. If he has had a few drinks too many, he may not realize what has happened. He may think it was a sudden attack of bursitis!

attack:

Same as in the previous move but this time your annoyer is wearing a heavy coat, buttoned, and you cannot reach his shoulder pressure points.

escape:

Using both hands, with your palms turned toward you and your fingers held straight and together, place the tip of the third or index finger to the hollow under the lobe of his ear. The hollow is between the jaw bone and the skull. Then apply pressure by pushing the fingers in and up toward each other and the top of his head. Do this move very gently in practice. Better yet, do it only on yourself and not on your practice partner.

8. NECK EMBRACE

attack:

Your attacker stands at your right with his arm over your shoulders or around your neck. It is not a dangerous attack, it is more like an embrace.

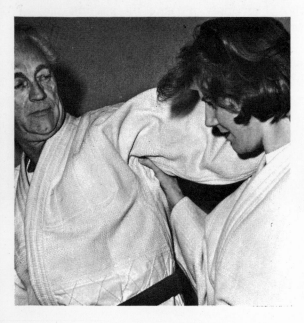

escape:

Hook the thumb of your right hand into his arm pit and curl your fingers round to encircle the muscle running up the back edge of his armpit. Apply the pinching motion. Keep knuckles bent and use the sides of the thumb and the fingers.

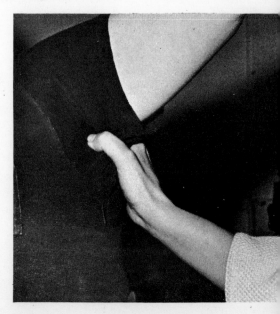

9. PUSH TO THE WALL

attack:

Your attacker holds you against the wall with his hands on your shoulders or at your neckline.

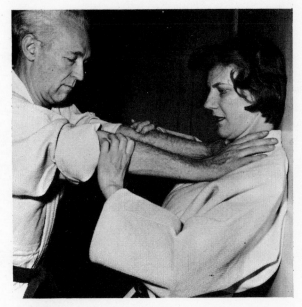

escape:

Reaching up, turn your hands toward each other and your fingertips on the tops of his forearm muscles at their largest point. Your thumbs apply pressure in the pinching motion from below. Move away when his grip weakens.

10. TWO HANDS TO ONE

attack:

Your opponent holds your right wrist with both of his hands in the normal manner, i.e., thumbs on opposite sides of your wrist and pointing down.

escape:

1. Step in between your opponent's feet with your right foot as you reach above and between his forearms with your left hand. Clenching your right fist, grasp it with your left hand. Keep both wrists straight.

2. Drive your right elbow in a semicircle in the Basic Hand Escape motion as you shift your weight forward onto your right foot. Keep your knees bent.

counter:

You can use the upward motion of your right elbow to strike his solar plexus, his jaw, or his nose, or you may prefer to strike back and down on his collarbone with the side of your right hand (methods described under counter-attacks for Basic Escapes). Practice again with the left hand.

Repeat again all of the preceding hand escapes, chokes, and counterattacks with each hand. Constant repetition will set these moves in your subconscious. In the event of a real attack, these reflexes should be automatic. Only conscientious practice will make them so.

11. BIM BAM BOOM

attack:

Your attacker chokes you with straight arms from the front as he pushes you against the wall.

escape:

1. Clasp your hands in front of your mouth. Do not interlace your fingers. Your right hand clasps the base of your left thumb.

2. If both your heels are against the wall, take half a step forward with your right foot. If your heels are away from the wall, take half a step back with your left foot. This will give you balance.

3. Hold your clasped hands in front of you, close to your mouth.

4. Pivot to your left on both feet. This will bring the back of your left hand sharply against his right wrist, close to the base of his right thumb.

5. Pivot back to your right and strike his left wrist close to the base of his left thumb.

6. Pivot back to face him and strike at his nose with your clasped hands. It is the pivoting action of your body that will free you. Do not slap at his wrists with wrist or arm motions. Your clasped hands must hold their position close to your mouth as your body pivots.

The purpose of this move is to use against the attacker the force with which he is pushing you. The harder he pushes you, the more vulnerable he becomes to this escape and counterattack. As you pivot rapidly, first to your left and then to your right, his push will make him fall forward as his hands slip from your neck. As he falls forward, your clasped hands striking forward sharply can break his nose. Bim is the blow to your left. Bam is the blow to your right. Boom, of course, is the blow to the nose. When you practice, please be careful with Boom.

12. COUNTERS TO A REAR ATTACK

attack:

Your attacker embraces you from the rear. His hands are clasped in front of you. He pins your arms to your sides at your elbows.

escape:

When he is holding you at elbow level, it is difficult to free yourself unless you first overset his balance. The first three moves are intended primarily to weaken your attacker by putting him off balance.

1. Raise your left knee high and drive your heel down into his left instep.

2. Raise your right knee high. Bend forward and drive your foot back into his right knee. This can dislocate his knee.

3. While you are still bent forward from the preceding move replace your right foot on the ground. Clasp your right wrist with your left hand. Straighten up rapidly and strike with the back of your head at his head. Careful when you practice this. You will strike his nose or his temple with the back of your head. His nose and temple are much more sensitive than the back of your head. If he anticipates this move, he will lean back to avoid you. This will still help you, for he is now standing with his weight on one foot and leaning in an off-balance position to his rear.

4. Bend forward again from the hips. Keep your back straight as you lean. As you bend, drive your hips back hard into his body. While still bent, bring your hands up in front of you (left hand still holds right wrist). Slightly raise your elbows sideways. Keep your wrists straight.

5. As you straighten your body upward, keep your arms locked in this position in relation to your body. Push your hips forward hard. This motion of your body with your arms locked shoulder-high will slide his arms up off your shoulders.

6. As soon as his arms are free of your shoulders, tuck your chin in, bend your knees a little more deeply, and in rapid succession strike at his short ribs (lower rib cage) with the back of your elbows. This motion, the Elbow Smash, is the one you have practiced for counterattacks. Pivot on the balls of both feet and strike to one side, then pivot and strike to the other side. Use the full force of the body, not just arm motion. The short ribs are the last few ribs on each side of the front rib cage. A blow here can collapse the lung, rendering the attacker unconscious. This will probably end the attack.

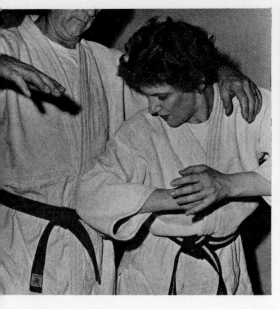

. Should he remain, pivot your right hip back and around so that your shoulders are at a right angle to the attacker. Your feet stay planted as you raise your hands shoulder-high, holding the fist of your right hand, in your left palm. Drive your right elbow back hard into his solar plexus.

8. Step back with your right foot just outside your attacker's left foot. Strike down with the outer edge of your right hand into the inside thigh muscle of his left leg.

practice:

In practice you may find it is difficult to free yourself until you have co-ordinated your body and arm motions. You must also keep in mind that you are not really stomping on your partner's foot or dislocating his knee, so he is not in as weakened a position as he would be in the event of a real attack. If he shifts his weight to one side, as an attacker would have to do, you will find it much easier to escape against this off-balance position. Be very careful that you do not actually hit, kick, or stomp on your partner as you practice.

If your attacker should hold your waist tightly from the rear under your arms, you can attack his head with your elbows, first twisting to your left and striking back and upward and then pivoting quickly to the other side and striking. You can also use the foot and knee attacks given above. If you like you can then take him down to the ground with the Low Pin (Move 35).

You may find it is only necessary to use the first or second move to free yourself. Once you are free you can take any action that is appropriate to the occasion.

13. WRIST LOCKS

We will now start working on Wrist Locks. Probably these will be your best weapon against most attacks, because they can be used in so many ways. It is important that you approach the lesson on Wrist Locks cautiously. A jerky motion can snap a wrist far more easily than you might think possible. All motion must be of a constant speed and consistent pressure.

To repeat, the sign of submission in Judo is two rapid slaps on yourself, on the mat, or on your partner. The hold must be released immediately when this sign is given. Be sure to slap loudly enough to be heard. For safety's sake your partner must not resist the lock. He must keep his wrist loose and relaxed. In a real attack your opponent's wrist is likely to be tense, and a tense wrist will break much more quickly than a relaxed wrist.

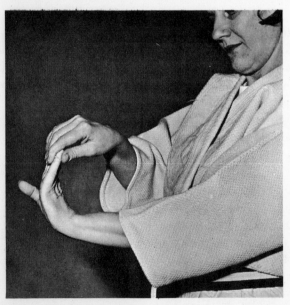

practice:

Hold your left arm in front of you, forearm parallel with the floor. Extend your fingers up, palm away from you. With your right hand pull the fingers of your left hand back toward you with a slow, steady pressure. Notice the tightening in the underpart of your left forearm. When you feel this tightening sensation, you should slap for submission. Do not wait for pain. Pain might come too late to prevent your wrist being broken. I suggest you watch your partner's free hand as you apply a lock. You can release your hold as soon as it starts to tap.

This is an exercise by which you learn to apply the position correctly and quickly. Stand facing your partner.

1. Grasp his right hand with your left hand. Place your left thumb, pointing down, on the back of his right hand. Wrap your fingers around the base of his thumb. Your fingers point in the same direction as your thumb.

2. With a counterclockwise twisting motion of your left hand, turn his hand so that the fingers point up.

3. Add your right hand in a similar position on the outside of his hand. Your thumbs should be parallel on the back of his hand.

4. Push with the pads of your thumbs against the back of his hand below his knuckles. Do not allow your thumbs to slip above the knuckles on to his fingers or you will lose most of your leverage. Your fingers pull toward you against the base of the palm of his hand close to his wrist. Your push-pull pressure should bring your fingers toward you until they are under your own thumbs. This is the basic Wrist Lock position.

5. In addition to bending your attacker's wrist toward him, you should rotate his wrist counterclockwise as though you were trying to touch his fingers to a spot about 3 inches outside his right elbow. Keep your elbows bent close to your body. Keep his forearm as parallel to the floor as possible. Do not lift his hand up close to his shoulder; keep it near belt level. When you think you are practicing slowly on this move—go still slower. Don't jerk the move.

6. Do this move several times against his left hand to familiarize yourself with the position. Then practice the same lock against his right hand. The motion is the same, except that your right hand will initiate the move against his left hand.

14. HAND ESCAPE TO LOCK

attack:

Your attacker holds your right wrist with his right hand. You have learned to escape from this grip, but if you feel your assailant intends to harm you, escaping is not the safest way to deal with him. It is better to control him or to break his wrist.

escape and lock:

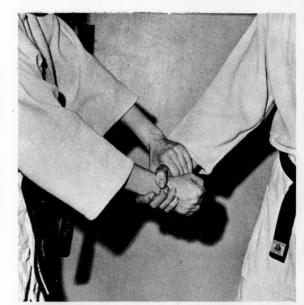

1. Grasp his right hand with your left hand in the Wrist Lock position—your left thumb against the back of his right hand with your fingers curled around the base of his right thumb.

2. Make a fist with your right hand. Keep your right wrist straight as you apply the lock with your left hand, bringing your right hand over his right wrist. This brings your forearm up almost parallel with your shoulders.

3. Increase the Wrist Lock pressure with your left hand as you turn slightly to your left.

4. Step in with your right foot as you turn. Push your right elbow forward until his hand releases its grip on your wrist.

5. Maintain contact between your right forearm and the back of his right hand as you slide your right hand down to join your left hand in the Wrist Lock position.

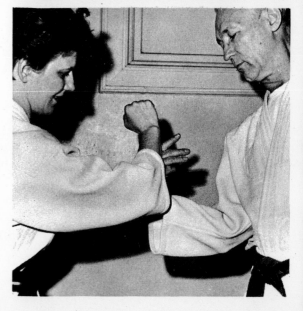

6. Apply the lock slowly until your partner slaps for submission. In the event of a real attack, apply the lock with a sharp, snapping motion to break his wrist. A Wrist Lock used only to escape from his grip might leave you vulnerable to a further attack. This technique can be used regardless of the position of his grip on your wrist. It is also an effective move against an attacker who is forcing your wrist down with a great deal of strength.

15. ALTERNATE WRIST LOCK

practice:

1. Stand facing your partner. Grasp his left hand with your left hand in Wrist Lock position, i.e., thumb pointing down on the back of his hand. Your fingers will be curled around the little-finger edge of his hand.

2. As you start to revolve your hand up in a counterclockwise motion, step around with your right foot so that you are to his left and behind him.

3. Add your right hand to the lock as you draw your left foot up to your right foot. Keep your elbows bent close to your waist. Keep your partner's arm straight by staying away from him; do not step in close to his rear.

4. Step to your right with your right foot, feet shoulder-width apart, knees slightly bent for balance. His fingers should now be pointing up, his arm straight.

5. Rotate his wrist counterclockwise as though you are trying to make his fingers touch a point about 3 inches outside his left elbow.

71

16. CROSS-HAND ESCAPE TO LOCK

attack:

Your attacker holds your right wrist with his left hand.

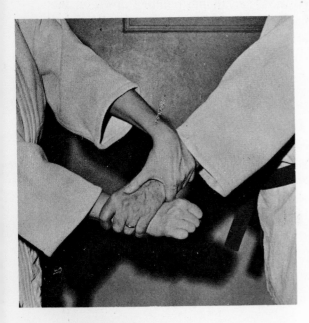

escape and lock:

1. Grasp his left hand with your left hand in Wrist Lock position, i.e., your left thumb against the back of his left hand with your fingers curled agound the little finger edge of his hand. Clench your right fist.

2. Keep your right wrist straight and right elbow bent as you apply the lock and step to his left and behind him with your right foot.

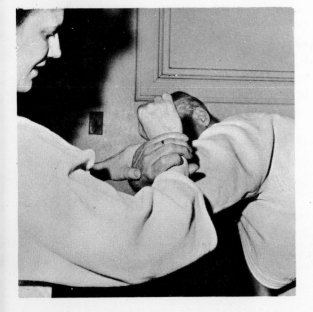

3. Bring your right fist up and over his left wrist as you turn and bring your left foot up to your right foot. This brings your right forearm up to shoulder height.

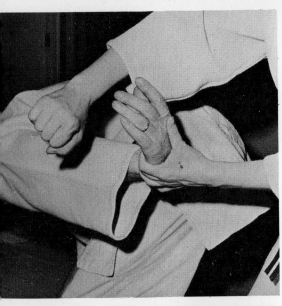

4. Take a step with your right foot and push your right elbow in to release your wrist from his grip as you increase the pressure of the lock with your left hand.

5. Add your right hand to the lock. Apply the lock with a slow, constant speed in practice.

6. In a real attack, apply the lock with a jerky, snapping motion to break the wrist. Notice the difference between a lock applied left hand against right hand and one applied left hand against left hand. Practice diligently with each hand against each of his hands.

17. FRONT CHOKE LOCK

As is the case with the preceding locks, while a simple escape will free you from a front choke, if it is necessary to control or incapacitate your attacker, the Front Choke Lock is your best weapon.

attack:

Your assailant chokes you from the front with his arms straight.

escape and lock:

1. Reach up between his hands with your right hand. Grasp his right hand with your right hand in the Wrist Lock position, i.e., right thumb on the back of his hand, fingers curled around the little-finger edge of his hand. Keep your wrist straight by raising your right elbow.

2. Turn your right heel in toward your left toes.

3. Simultaneously push with your thumb and lift with your fingers as you drop your right elbow. This lifts his hand from your neck. At the same time, with your left palm facing away from you—fingers straight and together, thumb making a V with the fore-finger—pivot to your right and direct a sharp blow at the underside of his right elbow with the V so made. The motions of your right and left hands should be made at the same time.

4. With your right hand still in the Wrist Lock position, keep his wrist bent as you pull his arm across in front of you, at the same time turning to your right.

74

5. Step in front of him with your left foot, close enough to bring your left rib cage in contact with his right rib cage. The palm of your left hand will push against his right elbow close to your waist. Your left elbow will be on his right shoulder blade. Your weight should be balanced equally on both feet. Keep him close to you. Stand erect, knees slightly bent. Allow your right thumb to slip around between his thumb and fingers. Use your lock on his wrist to keep his body close to yours and his arm in close contact with your waist. Keep your left wrist straight and your left hand close to the center of your waist. Your left hand should keep a constant down pressure on his right elbow.

6. To apply the lock, push your hips to your right as you raise your right elbow. Do not bend your body forward. You are now applying pressure against three joints: his wrist, elbow, and shoulder. You can break any of the three joints; the choice is yours.

18. TAKEDOWN

You can also use the last move of the Front Choke Lock to take your attacker to the ground. From the lock position, controlling his body by controlling his arm, drop to your left knee. Folding your left foot under you, sit down with your right leg bent. Continue to hold your lock. Your attacker will be lying face down. If he struggles or attempts to kick or pull away, increase the pressure of the lock. Keep your right hand locking his wrist and pull his arm to your right. You can incapacitate your attacker by breaking a joint or hold him if help is on the way.

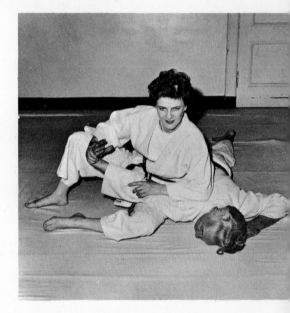

19. KICKS

Your feet can be a powerful weapon when used correctly. Here is one simple type of kick. When you kick out from a standing position, the action can upset your balance. To maintain your balance best, lean away from your target. For practice purposes choose as your target a spot on the wall about knee-high. Stand about 2½ feet away from the wall, facing your target. Turn 90 degrees to your left, so that your right side is toward the wall. Bend both knees slightly and lean about 45 degrees to your left. For balance in the beginning, lean on a chair with your left hand: Draw your right knee up as close to your chest as possible. Curl your toes up and strike with your foot at the target, *slowly*. Do not kick with your toe. Aim the bottom of your foot at the target. You must use the thigh muscle, not the calf muscle. The kick should be a bouncing motion, as though your thigh muscle were a spring. As soon as your leg straightens in the kick, pull your knee right back up to your chest, ready to strike again. Do not snap the kick when you are first practicing.

practice:

Have your partner hold his hand about knee-high. Turn to your left, lean, and kick against his hand with your right foot; then turn, lean, and kick with your left foot. Remember to bend away from your target and to use only your thigh muscle for kicking.

20. REAR BENT-ARM CHOKE
WITH KICK

attack:

Your assailant chokes you from the rear. His elbows are bent and he is standing close to you. If his arms are straight, it is better to use another escape, the Basic Rear Choke Escape (Move 5). To make sure that his arms are bent, look or reach up with your hands to feel his elbows or forearms.

escape and counter:

1. Keeping the fingers together, reach up with both hands and press your thumbs against the little-finger edge of his hands. Drive your fingers between his little fingers and ring fingers. Grab his little fingers with your fingers as you increase the pressure of your thumbs.

2. Release his hold on your throat by applying a lock on his little fingers. Maintain your hold on his little fingers and raise your elbows to increase the pressure of the thumbs. This takes his hands from your throat.

3. Step obliquely forward and to your right with your right foot. Bend slightly forward, knees slightly bent, as you shift your weight onto your right foot. At the same time, duck your head and lift his right arm over your head and down across your body. Maintain your lock on his little fingers as you lean to your right.

4. Using your lock on his little fingers to maintain your balance, pull him forward. Raise your left knee and kick at your attacker's right knee.

KNIFE ATTACKS

We will now start our study of knife attacks. If your assailant has a knife or a gun and he demands money, give him the money. Money can always be replaced; it is not as easy to replace vital parts of your body. But if someone should attack you with a knife, you must try to defend yourself. At the very instant that you see a knife in your assailant's hand, bend your elbows and raise your hands close to your chest. Your fingers should be extended and together, ready to strike if you must. In this first glance, you must notice how the knife is held. If the blade extends from the little-finger edge of the hand, the attack will most likely come from above or from across his chest. If the blade extends from the thumb side of his hand, the attack will probably come from below in a sweeping motion or straight toward your body in a stabbing motion. The first rule in the event of a knife attack is to keep your body out of the path of the knife. At the start your partner should strike at a slow, steady speed. This will enable you to set your rhythm. It is not the speed with which you defend yourself that counts but the rhythm with which you move. Do not practice with a real knife; you may use a rubber knife, if you like.

21. KNIFE SLASH

attack:

Your attacker holds the knife with the blade extending from the little-finger edge of his right hand. He lifts his right forearm across his chest, shoulder-high. His right hand is close to his left shoulder. He slashes out, straightening his arm, toward your heart.

escape and lock:

1. As he starts his slashing move, step obliquely forward and to the left with your left foot. Pivot 90 degrees to your right as you raise your hands in front of your eyes, about shoulder-width apart. Palms face each other; fingers are together, wrists straight. This puts your forearms and hands in a position to block the slashing motion of his right arm. Your position should be at a right angle to your attacker's. Your left foot is close to and pointing at your attacker's right foot. Do not attempt to strike at your assailant's striking arm. Instead, by making the movements described, step outside his line of attack, and let your attacker's arm complete its swing. His arm should be straight when it comes in contact with your blocking arms. Your knees will be bent. If your assailant is your height or taller, your knees will be bent only slightly for balance. If your assailant is shorter than you, you must bend your knees deeply enough to be able to block his slashing motion with the center of your forearms. Your right forearm will make contact with his right wrist. Your left forearm will be just above his elbow.

2. As soon as his arm strikes your blocking forearms, slide your right hand down. Keeping contact with his right wrist, slide your right thumb under his wrist and grab the wrist. Turn the knife away from you. Keep his arm straight with an outward pull to your right side.

3. Simultaneously, step in front of your assailant with your left foot. Your left forearm will maintain a steady pressure on the pressure point just above his right elbow. Pull his arm, which must be kept straight, close to your waist with your right hand. Your left forearm will now be extending straight forward from your left hip. Your weight should be on the balls of both feet, your knees slightly bent.

4. To apply the lock, use your straight left forearm as a bar. The forearm bone on the outside of the forearm should be applied to the pressure point just above his elbow. Raise your right elbow and shift your hips to your right. Do not bend your body to the front. When he attacks with a knife don't hesitate—break his arm.

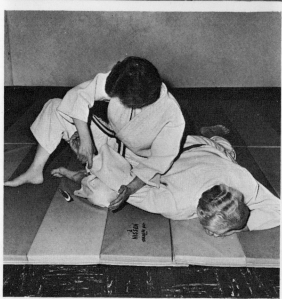

5. Maintaining the pressure exerted by your hands and arms, sink down onto your left knee. Folding your left foot under you, sit down with your right knee bent.

   This move is very similar to the lock from a front choke (Move 17). The main difference is the position of your left arm and the contact of your body with the assailant's. In the Front Choke Lock position your left rib cage is in close contact with his right rib cage and your left forearm is roughly parallel with your body. In this move your body is not in contact with his, and your left forearm is at right angles to your body. The shift of weight to your right is the same as in the Front Choke Lock. A snapping motion up with your right hand will break his elbow.

22. KNIFE ATTACK FROM ABOVE—RIGHT SIDE

attack:

Your attacker holds the knife in his right hand with the blade extending from the little-finger edge of his hand. He raises his right hand above his right shoulder and strikes down at you.

escape and lock:

1. As he strikes down, step in with your right foot toward your attacker, pivot to your left, and raise your right arm to above shoulder height, so that the forearm blocks the blow. Your body now should be parallel to the path of the knife. His striking forearm will hit your blocking forearm.

2. After you have blocked his blow, grasp his right wrist with your right hand, and, driving your left hand under his right arm, grasp your own right wrist with your left hand, palm facing away from you.

84

3. Step in with your left foot as your left hand moves.

4. Step behind his right leg with your right foot. By raising your left elbow you exert pressure that can break his elbow.

5. To take your assailant to the ground, bend forward. Your attacker's leg is blocked by your leg, so when he is off balance he will fall. Maintain your lock on his arm and sink onto your right knee.

6. Apply pressure on the lock to make him drop the knife or to break his elbow.

23. KNIFE ATTACK FROM ABOVE—LEFT SIDE

attack:

Your attacker holds the knife in his right hand with the blade extending from the little-finger edge of the hand. He raises his right hand above his right shoulder and strikes down at you. Your left side is turned toward your attacker when he strikes down at you.

escape and lock:

1. Step in close to your assailant's right side with your left foot, planting it close to your attacker's right foot. Simultaneously, raise your left to above shoulder height to block the blow with the forearm.

2. Bend your right knee and lean to the right, keeping your head away from the knife. Your body should be parallel to the path of the blow.

3. Driving your right hand under his arm, move your right foot up to your left foot. Keep your knees slightly bent and your body at right angles to his. Grab your left wrist with your right hand, palm away from you.

4. Take another step to your left with your left foot, knees slightly bent. Bring your elbows in close to your body at the waist. It is important in this technique that you keep your body turned at right angles to your attacker's throughout the move. You should be facing directly toward his right side, as though you were looking in his right ear. Keep both wrists straight. Your left hand should be in front of his right shoulder. You may grasp his clothes at the front of the shoulder with your left hand if you like.

5. Exerting pressure down with your left forearm while using your right elbow as a fulcrum will knock him off balance backward and drive him to the ground. You can make him drop the knife or break his elbow by raising your right elbow. An alternate lock that will separate his arm from his shoulder joint may be applied by raising your right elbow while you are standing.

practice:

Practice the foot and body motions by yourself first. Then add the arm and hand positions.

24. KNIFE ATTACK FROM BELOW

attack:

Your attacker holds the knife in his right hand with the blade extending from the thumb side of the hand. He swings up from below, or jabs straight in, toward your stomach.

escape and lock:

1. As your assailant starts his attack, step obliquely forward and to the left with your left foot and pivot to your right. Simultaneously, strike down with your left hand directly in front of your left hipbone, with your left elbow held close to your side. The movement of your body to outside his striking path should bring his wrist directly in front of you as you strike. Your blow should hit just a little above his right wrist. This may cause him to drop the knife. In any case, drop your left hand onto his right hand in Wrist Lock position.

2. As you shift your weight back to your right foot, pivot to face your assailant and add your right hand to the lock on his wrist.

3. As you take a step back with your left foot, turn 90 degrees to your left. Increasing the pressure of the lock on his wrist, pull the wrist sharply down to your left knee. The lock on his wrist will cause him to fall in front of you.

4. Maintain the lock as he falls to control him. Break the wrist with a sharp snap as you throw. Do not actually throw your partner unless he can fall.

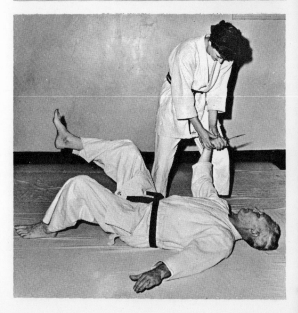

25. KNIFE ATTACK FROM BELOW—LIMITED AREA

attack:

Your attacker holds the knife in his right hand with the knife extending from the thumb side of the hand. He swings up from below, or jabs straight in, toward your stomach. This is the same attack as in the previous move, but this time you are in a small area, such as a hallway or an elevator.

escape and lock:

1. Cross your wrists, right over left, palms down, in front of you and draw your hips well back to avoid the blow. The attacker's arm will be caught between your crossed wrists.

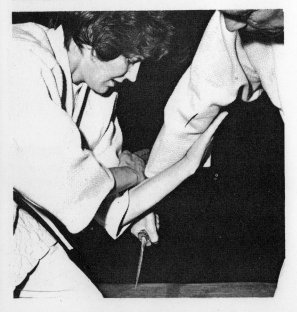

2. Turn your left palm up and slide your left hand up to behind your attacker's right elbow. Maintain pressure against his wrist with your right wrist.

3. Step around behind your attacker with your left foot, knees slightly bent. Simultaneously, push his elbow down and to your right with your left hand. This bends his right elbow and places his arm in an Arm Lock.

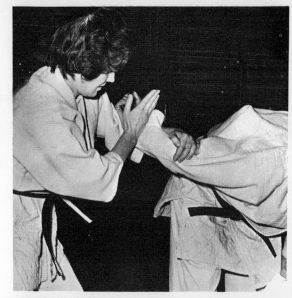

4. His right wrist is trapped in the crook of your left arm against your left bicep.

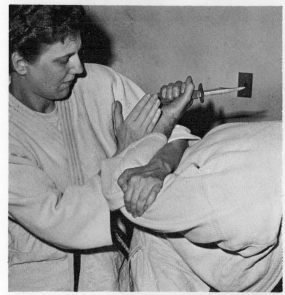

5. Reach over with your right hand, grasp the hand holding the knife, and apply a Wrist Lock by pulling the hand toward your right. This will make him drop the knife. If he does not, you are in a position to break his wrist. Grasping his collar with your right hand will give you better control. By raising your left elbow you can break his elbow, drive him head first into the wall, or walk him to the nearest police station.

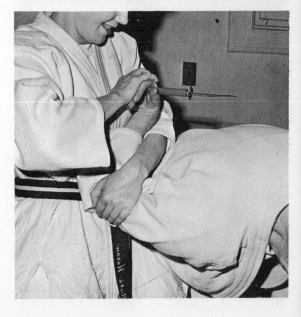

FIST ATTACKS

Women rarely are involved in fistfights, but we never know when we may have to defend ourselves against a punch from a frustrated attacker.

26. STRAIGHT RIGHT PUNCH TO THE HEAD

attack:

Your attacker punches at your head with a straight right-hand punch from a distance of 3 or 4 feet.

escape and lock:

1. Step obliquely forward and to your left as you deflect his arm upward with your left hand. Keep your chin tucked into your left shoulder.

2. Drive your right hand over his left shoulder as you step behind his right foot with your right foot. The thumb edge of your right wrist should be against his neck—(views are from both sides.)

3. Step forward with your left foot as you grasp your right wrist with your left hand, left thumb under right wrist. His right arm is now trapped between your head and your right shoulder. Keep your head against his raised arm to hold it tightly. Keep both of your wrists straight. Your feet should be about shoulder-width apart with your knees slightly bent.

4. To apply the lock, squeeze your hands toward your mouth. Continue to clench your right hand, palm down.

5. To take your attacker to the ground, drop to your right knee. Maintain your lock as you sink. Keep your right shoulder against his upper arm and lean into it to separate the arm from the shoulder. (Views are from both sides.)

27. ROUNDHOUSE PUNCH TO THE HEAD

attack:

Your attacker throws a roundhouse punch or a hook at your head from a distance of about 3 feet.

escape and counter:

1. Step obliquely back and to the left, turn to your left, bend forward, and raise your right arm to block his blow with the forearm.

2. Grasp his sleeve or arm with your right hand as you lean to your left. Pull him toward you with your right hand to break his balance diagonally forward and to his right.

3. Raise your right knee up close to your chest and kick at his right knee.

28. TWO HANDS TO ONE—CLOSED

attack:

Your attacker holds your right wrist with both of his hands, thumbs on opposite sides of your wrist and pointing down. This resembles the attack in Two Hands to One (Move 10), except that this time his forearms are close together.

escape:

1. Make a fist with your right hand. Reach over your attacker's wrists and grab your right fist with your left hand.

2. Step obliquely forward and to the right oblique with your right foot. Drive your right elbow under your attacker's hands.

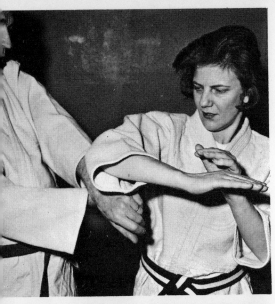

3. When your hands are shoulder-high, raise your right elbow shoulder-high and pivot to your left as you pull your hands to your left shoulder. This frees you from his grip.

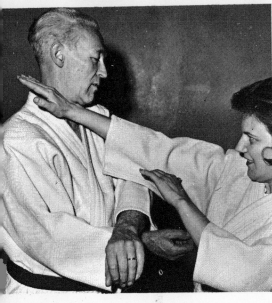

4. Your counterattack will be a blow with your right hand to the right side of his neck or with your right elbow (clenched right fist clasped in left hand) to his jaw.

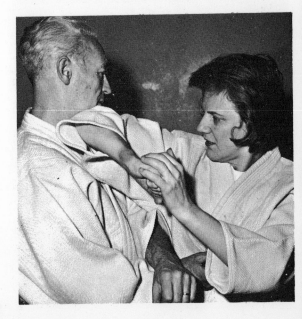

29. TWO HANDS UP

attack:

Your attacker is holding both of your wrists with both of his hands, thumbs up. Your elbows are down and your hands are up, palms facing each other. Your forearms are vertical and parallel.

escape:

1. Make fists with both hands. As you step in between your attacker's feet with your right foot, turn both forearms so that your fists come down toward each other and your elbows rise to shoulder height.

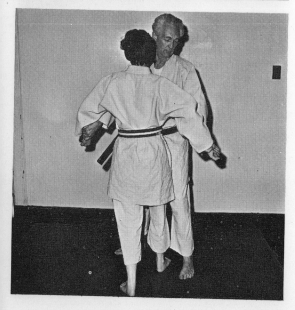

2. Continue to bring both hands down in this circular motion as your weight shifts forward onto your right foot.

3. Straighten your arms out to the side at shoulder height, palms up. This should free you from his grip. If your attacker's arms are longer than yours and he retains his hold on your wrists at this point, turn each of your hands palm up, as though you were hitching a ride with the thumbs.

4. Continue the motion of your body forward into your attacker's. Your chest hits your attacker's chest and knocks him backward off balance. This will preclude the possibility of his grabbing your body with his hands or arms.

5. Your hands can be raised and brought down on your attacker's collarbone in a counterblow.

30. CLUB ATTACK

attack:

Your attacker raises a club and strikes down toward your head. The club is in his right hand.

escape and lock:

1. Step obliquely forward and to the left with your left foot as you raise your right arm and block his right forearm with your right forearm.

2. Pivot to your right as you slide your right hand down his right forearm to his wrist and grasp his wrist with your thumb under the wrist while your fingers apply pressure on the back of his hand. Slide your right foot up to your left foot.

3. Take a step to your left with your left foot and swing his hand toward your waist by increasing the pressure of the lock on his wrist. Keep his arm straight. Do not allow him to bend his elbow. If his elbow bends, it means you are too close to him. You should be about 3 feet diagonally behind and to the right of the point of his right shoulder.

4. Shift your weight to your left foot as your right hand swings up to your waist.

5. With your left hand, grasp the club just above his grip and twist the club to your right (clockwise). Continue the lock on his wrist with your right hand.

101

6. If the occasion warrants it, you can strike him on the back of his head with the club held in your left hand, retaining the lock with your right hand.

31. LAPEL GRIP

attack:

Your attacker grabs your left lapel or shirt front with his right hand, thumb up.

escape and lock:

1. Seize your attacker's right wrist with your left hand. Your fingers will encircle his wrist and your thumb will be applied to the the back of his hand for leverage. If he turns his hand inward to hide his thumb, you can turn it outward again by dropping your left elbow as you push with your thumb and pull with your fingers.

2. Turning your shoulders to the right, place the base of your right thumb on top of his right thumb The position of your shoulders and right arm and hand is similar to an archer's position as he prepares to shoot an arrow from his bow.

3. Slide your right hand toward your chest until the tip of his thumb is just at the base of your thumb. Wrap your fingers around the side of his hand at the base of his thumb.

103

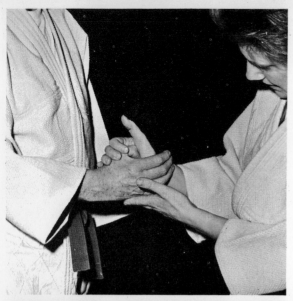

4. With your right hand squeeze your fingers toward your thumb, as though you were making a fist. This will apply a lock on either the first or second thumb joint, depending upon whether you apply your pressure down with the base of your thumb (applies pressure to the second joint) or up (applies pressure to the first joint). As you squeeze to apply the lock, you also push his hand off your clothes, keeping both your hands in position.

5. When his hand is free of your clothes, you may break his thumb or release your right-hand lock on his thumb.

6. Immediately add your right hand to the lock your left hand has on his right wrist. Then you may break his wrist.

7. You can throw him to the ground, as in Knife Attack from Below (Move 24), by stepping back with your left foot, pivoting to the left through a 90-degree angle, and increasing the pressure on the lock, pulling the wrist sharply down to your left knee. Maintain the lock as he falls. Do not throw your partner unless he knows how to fall.

32. LAPEL GRIP—
TAKEDOWN

attack:

Your attacker grabs your left lapel or shirt front with his right hand.

escape and takedown:

1. Seize your attacker's right wrist with your right hand, thumb under his wrist.

2. Pull his hand in to your chest and hold his hand to your chest with your left hand.

3. Step back with your left foot and pivot to your left, still holding his hand tightly against your chest. Bend forward from your hips as you turn and bend your knees.

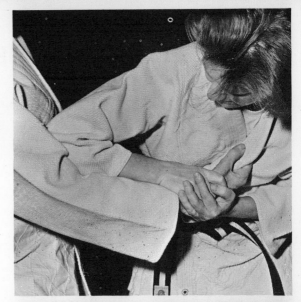

4. Your bent right elbow and forearm press against the inside of his right forearm.

5. The combined action of your right arm's pressure against his right arm and the forward bending of your body will throw him down to the mat. Be gentle with your partner.

ADVANCED ESCAPES

33. HAND ESCAPE—
INVERTED GRIP

attack:

Your attacker holds your right wrist with his left hand in an inverted position, i.e., thumb down on the outside of your wrist.

escape:

1. Step to your right with your right foot. Raise your elbow to the side as you bring your fist over his wrist.

2. Turn to your left with your forearm at shoulder height. This releases your wrist.

3. Deliver a counterblow with your right hand to your attacker's neck or nose. This escape will also work against an attacker holding your wrist in the normal position but also pushing your arm down.

When you have developed excellent coordination you can use the Advanced Hand Escape (page 110).

34. ADVANCED HAND ESCAPE

attack:

Attacker is holding your right wrist with his left hand in the normal position.

escape:

1. Using your right elbow as a fulcrum, snap your right wrist round and up to the outside of your right shoulder. Drive the thumb side of your wrist out of the space between his thumb and fingers with a twist of the wrist, as though you were hitchhiking.

2. Continue the motion of your right arm upward.

3. Deliver a counterblow with your right hand to the collarbone.

35. LOW PIN

In this move you will take your opponent to the ground. Because of the danger of injury to your partner while you practice, some precautions must be taken. You might recruit a third person to help. Have him stand behind your partner with his hands under your partner's arms. He should be prepared to catch your partner as he falls backwards. If there is no third person available, you might try the movement slowly in front of an easy chair (not a hard wooden or metal chair). Your partner should keep his chin on his chest to prevent his head from snapping back. Of course, if your partner is adept in the art of falling and you have a mat for him to fall on, there is no problem.

attack:

Your partner embraces you from the rear. His hands are clasped in front of you. He pins your arms to your sides *below* the elbow.

escape and counter:

1. Straighten your hands, palms against your body, bend your elbows, and slide your hands up one at a time to free your arms.

2. Step to your right so that his right foot is between your feet. Bending your knees slightly, bend forward and place your left hand on the ground in front of you.

3. Place your right hand behind his right heel and pull it toward your left hand with a sharp, jerky motion.

4. When his foot is off the ground, straighten up and with both hands pull his foot up toward your abdomen. Keep your shoulders hunched forward to maintain your balance. As he falls he will probably release you. He will probably hit his head on the ground as he falls.

5. If he does not release you, straighten your back and sit hard on his abdomen. Keep your hold on his foot and add your other hand to apply a lock against his ankle. Pull sharply toward your waist to break his ankle.

36. ARM LOCK

As we practiced Wrist Lock positions before we learned how to use them, so we must practice and learn the best position for applying an arm lock.

practice:

1. Stand facing your partner. Place the V made by your left thumb and fingers palm up against your partner's right wrist as you step to his right side with your left foot.

2. Grasp the sleeve or arm above his right elbow with your right hand, thumb down.

3. Move your right foot up to your left foot as you push his wrist up with your left hand and pull with your right hand.

4. Step round closely behind him with your left foot. Slide your left arm under his wrist and grasp his arm or sleeve above the right elbow with your left hand. It is important that his wrist stays securely placed against your left bicep. Stay in close so that his elbow lies against your front rib cage.

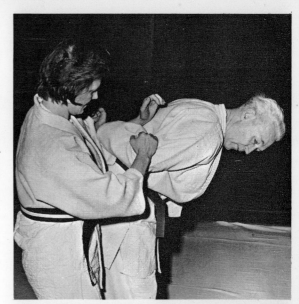

5. Move your right hand up to grasp his left shoulder, his collar at the back, or his hair. If he has no hair, you can achieve a very effective lock by straightening your right index finger, placing it under his nose, and forcing his head back.

37. TWO HANDS IN BACK

attack:

Your assailant stands behind you and holds your wrists behind your back. His right hand holds your right wrist and his left hand holds your left wrist in the normal position, i.e., thumbs pointing up inside your wrists.

escape and lock:

1. Step diagonally back and to your right to the outside of your attacker's body, so that your right hip comes in close contact with your right hand and arm. Keep your right arm held against your right side.

2. Step back behind your attacker with your left foot as you bend forward. This slides his right arm over your head.

3. Straighten up. He may release his hold at this point.

4. If he continues to hold your wrists, grab the back of his right arm above the elbow with your left hand. By moving your right hand over your left forearm you are placing them in an Arm Lock position. Your right wrist can be easily released at this point by snapping your right wrist up toward your right shoulder.

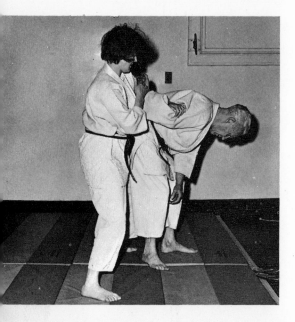

5. You may then use the Arm Lock to break his arm, control him, or to walk him to wherever you wish.

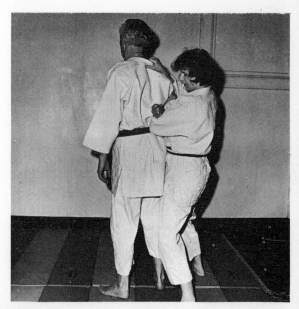

38. MUGGING ESCAPE

attack:

Your assailant throws his right arm around your neck from behind. He may clasp his hands on your left shoulder.

escape and counter:

1. Reach up with both of your hands and grasp his right wrist with your hands close together, thumbs under his wrist. Hold his wrist tightly against your chest so that it will have to move with your body.

2. Turn your chin to your left shoulder and tuck it in tightly against your chest.

3. Step to your right with your right foot.

4. Pivot to your left and bend forward.

5. Step back with your left foot, still bending, and drive your body and head back under your attacker's right arm.

6. Continue holding his wrist against your chest.

7. Stand erect and apply a Wrist Lock against your attacker's right wrist (Move 15).

8. Depending upon circumstances, you may break his wrist so that he is incapacitated and cannot harm you. If circumstances warrant, you may swing your right foot forward and kick him in the face, or go from the Wrist Lock to an Arm Lock by stepping in close behind him, sliding your left arm under his wrist to grasp his arm or sleeve above the elbow, and using your right hand either to pull his head back or to grasp his collar (Move 36).

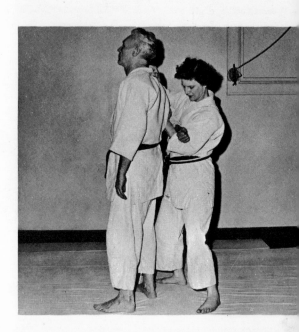

39. SLEEVE GRIP

attack:

You and your attacker are standing side by side. He is at your right. He holds or pulls your right upper outer sleeve with his left hand.

escape and lock:

1. Make a fist with your right hand to keep your wrist straight.

2. Swing your right fist up and over his left arm from the front. The thumb edge of your fist should make contact with the back of his arm just above his elbow.

3. Step in with your right foot parallel to his left foot and close to it. Keep your body in line with his and facing in the same direction. As you step in, bend your right elbow and with your right wrist push his elbow forward. This motion traps his left wrist under your right armpit. Your right arm holds his left forearm tightly against your right side.

4. Place your left palm under your right fist to support your lock.

5. Your right wrist should be applying pressure just slightly above his left elbow.

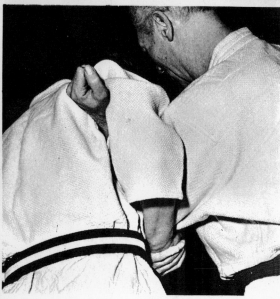

6. If your attacker should attempt to strike at you with his other hand, lean back and bring your hands up to apply the lock.

7. The swinging arm motion and lock must be smooth and continuous.

8. Practice the move slowly and carefully with your opponent first on your right, then on your left.

40. COME-ALONG

This move can be used to walk someone out of a crowded area or to control someone who is causing a disturbance. It can also be used in an automobile or theatre against a molester, as in the following attack.

attack:

A molester places his left hand on your knee when you are sitting side by side.

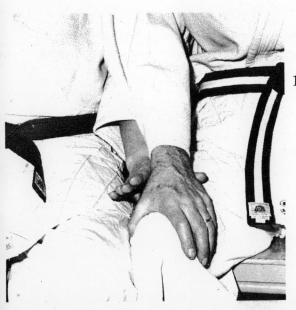

lock:

1. With your right hand held palm down, fingers together and thumb extended away from the hand, move your right arm under his left arm, place your right thumb under his wrist, grasp the back of his hand with your fingers, and bend his hand downward.

2. With your left hand push his left bicep back to trap his left arm under your right armpit.

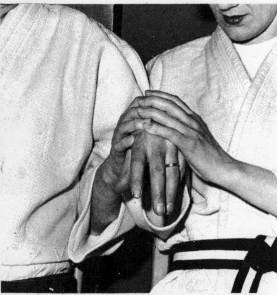

3. Add your left hand to the lock on his wrist in the same position as your right hand.

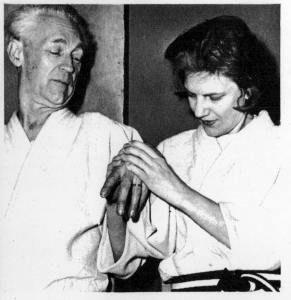

4. Bring his wrist up toward your shoulder to apply the lock. Thumbs push up and fingers pull in.

5. If the molester attempts to strike you with his free hand, lean back and apply the lock harder.

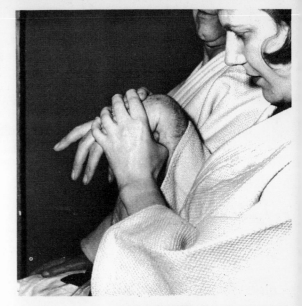

6. From a standing or walking position, this lock can be applied by sliding your right arm under his left arm. Grasp his hand with your right hand and push his arm back with your left hand, as described in stages 1 and 2.

7. Apply the lock by pulling his wrist up toward your shoulder. Keep your body side by side with his.

41. ELBOW LOCK

attack:

Sitting beside you on your right, your molester places his left hand on your right knee.

lock:

1. Grab his right wrist with your left hand and hold it down on your knee and in toward your body.

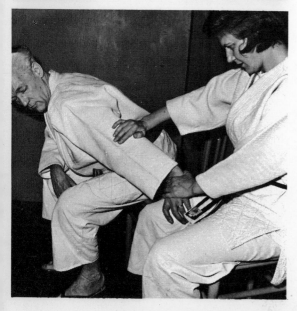

2. Strike behind his left elbow with your right hand and push.

3. By keeping his arm straight and exerting pressure against his elbow, you can drive your molester forward on his face onto the floor, or if he resists, break his elbow.

4. If you prefer, in order to control him, you can bend his arm and apply an Arm Lock (Move 36).

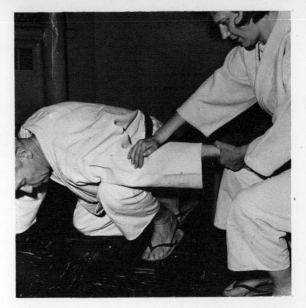

42. PUSH-ALONG

This is an ejecting move. If someone creates a disturbance and you wish to eject him, the Come-Along (Move 40) works very effectively. If he happens to be the bully type who might return to cause further trouble, as soon as you have ejected him, the following move is intended to embarrass him and make him look ridiculous. Under these circumstances it is not likely he would return to the scene of his humiliation. In this situation you are not being attacked but decide to eject someone before trouble starts.

1. Stand facing your partner's left side as calmly and nonchalantly as possible.

2. In a rather quick motion with your left hand, grasp his left wrist—thumb on the inside of his wrist—and lean forward, pushing his hand down between his legs. Supplement this push with a push down on his back just below the shoulders with your right hand.

3. Reach between his legs from the rear with your right hand, grasp his left wrist, and pull his wrist up between his legs. Let go of your hold with your left hand.

4. Grasp his collar or the back of his coat with your left hand.

5. Coordinate the actions of your hands—lifting with your right hand and pushing or pulling with your left hand. Push him forward in the direction in which you wish to send him.

6. He will have to move forward to avoid falling on his face. If you lift too hard with your right hand, he will fall. Counter this action by holding firmly with your left hand.

43. ARM LOCK ESCAPE

attack:

Your attacker grasps your right arm and applies an Arm Lock to it.

escape and counter takedown:

1. To prevent your attacker from breaking your elbow in the first snapping motion, grasp a handful of your own clothing as your arm is swung into the lock position.

2. Step forward with your left foot half a step. Bend straight forward toward your left knee. Release your grip with your right hand and straighten your arm as though you were throwing a straight punch back and down with your right fist.

3. Pivot on both feet, knees bent, 180 degrees to face your attacker, still bent forward. Your right hand now will be close to the outside of your attacker's left knee.

4. Bring your left hand to the outside of your attacker's right knee. Your right shoulder will be against the front of your attacker's hips as though you were tackling him.

5. Grasp the trousers behind his knees with each hand and pull in toward your knees as you lean forward, pushing his hips backward with your right shoulder. He will fall backward hard. In a street attack he will probably strike his head on the sidewalk. Do not actually throw your partner in practice unless he has been trained in falling techniques.

44. HEAD LOCK ESCAPE

This is a fairly common type of attack in a street brawl. Normally it would not be used as an initial attack upon a woman, but in a scuffle you might find yourself in this position.

attack:

Your partner stands at your left with his right arm around your neck. He holds his right wrist with his left hand and his grip forces you to bend forward. He is not trying to harm you, merely to hold you. If you wish to escape from his grip the following method will apply. In practice, he should not hold your neck too tightly while you are learning the correct position and body movement.

escape and counter:

1. Turn your chin far to the left and tuck it into your chest.

2. Grasp his right sleeve at the elbow with your right hand, palm down. Grasp his right upper sleeve with your left hand, palm down. Place your left foot in back of and inside his right foot. Your left knee will push into the back of his right knee or against the outside of his calf.

3. Simultaneously, kneel down and forward with your left knee and push his arm off over your head. Duck your head and straighten your body.

4. If you push straight forward with your hands on his sleeve as you kneel strongly downward on the back of his right leg, your attacker will fall on his face.

45. HEAD LOCK TAKEDOWN

attack:

Your partner stands at your left with his right arm around your neck, forcing you to bend forward, as in the previous move. Suppose that in this instance the attack may be dangerous and you must incapacitate the attacker to safeguard yourself.

escape and takedown:

1. Grasp the back of his right knee or his trousers at the outside of the right knee with your right hand, palm toward his knee. Reach up round his neck and grasp his left shoulder with your left hand, fingers pointing down against the front of his shoulder.

2. Simultaneously, lift his right leg up and forward with your right hand, pull back and down with your left hand, and pivot around (about face). Make an 180-degree turn.

3. Your partner will fall on his left side in front of you.

4. He will usually release his grip on your neck when he feels himself falling. If he should maintain his hold on your neck, bring your knee up and kneel on his right kidney. Do not actually kneel on your partner's kidney as you may injure his kidney, which is extremely painful. Use either knee.

5. With both hands grasp his sleeve at the elbow with your right hand and on the upper arm with your left hand, as in the preceding move, and slip his arm over your head as you straighten your body up.

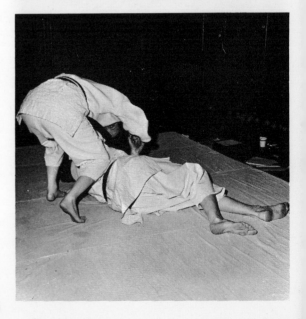

46. PURSE-SNATCHER TAKEDOWN

attack:

The attacker runs past you in either direction and takes your purse from your right hand as he passes you.

takedown:

1. If he is unarmed, raise your right hand quickly and grasp his collar, hair, or shoulder, as you pivot and lean to your left and kick behind his closest knee with your right foot.

2. Pull sharply down with your right hand. This is a very hard fall, so do not actually throw your partner unless he can fall well.

3. Practice the move with your left hand.

47. FRONT MEDIUM PIN

attack:

Your attacker grabs you from the front with a bear hug, pinning your arms to your body above the elbows.

escape and takedown:

1. Reach in under his elbows with your hands and grasp the back of his coat at each side. Pull him in close to you. Place your right foot between his feet and behind his left foot. Hook your right heel behind his left heel. Block the backward motion of his left foot with your right foot.

2. Lean in with your right shoulder against his chest and push down with hands and shoulder as you shift your weight forward onto your right foot. Right knee bends deeply. This will drive him straight down on his back.

Do not throw your partner unless he can fall. If he has not been trained in falling techniques you can sit your partner down with a slow, gentle motion.

Usually the attacker will release you when he feels himself falling backward. If he should not release you after he lands on the ground, kneel in to his groin area with your right knee and straighten your body up and back.

48. GROUND ESCAPE

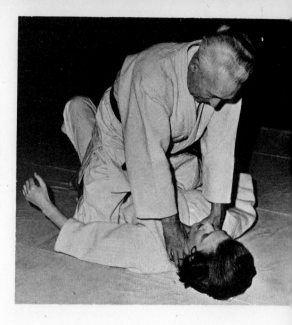

attack:

You are in a prone position with your attacker kneeling astride your body. He chokes you with his bare hands; his arms are straight; his weight bears down on your throat. The attacker may have knocked you down or assaulted you while you were lying down.

escape:

1. Raise your knees. Your feet are flat on the mat. Hook your fingers rigidly inside the attacker's wrists from above.

2. With a short, sharp, jerky motion pull each wrist to the outside, off your neck.

3. As soon as his right hand releases your neck, move your left forearm up against his right forearm to prevent him from reaching forward with his right hand to support himself. Place your right hand under his left rib cage.

4. His body will fall forward. Use this momentum to carry him off your body.

5. Raise your hips to arch your body. Turn your shoulders to your left and throw him over your left shoulder with your right hand. All of these moves must be continuous, without any hesitation between them. Keep his body moving forward. Your attacker will probably hit his head or the top of his shoulder on the ground. To roll safely, your partner should tuck his head in and roll over as in a somersault. If you are attacked while in bed, this is an effective move.

49. BASIC HIP THROW— OGOSHI

This is a basic Judo throw that can be used against many different attacks. It is to be practiced by students only under an instructor's supervision and after they have gained proficiency in throwing and falling.

1. Stand facing your partner. Grasp the back of his upper right sleeve with your left hand.

2. Step in with your right foot just inside and slightly in front of his right foot. Pull gently with your left arm—raised shoulder-high, elbow bent—as you turn, so as to bring his weight forward onto the toes of his right foot.

3. Bend your knees slightly and pivot your body to the left in front of his body as you put your right arm around his waist under his left arm. Place the palm on his back; do not hold his coat.

4. Move your left foot up to your right foot, heels in line and fairly close together, toes slightly turned out. Bend your knees out away from each other about shoulder-width apart.

5. You should now be standing in front of your attacker, your body parallel with his and touching it from the hips up to your armpit. Your back must be straight, not hunched or rounded. Your hips must be lower than his hips. Tuck your chin in.

6. Push your hips back and up as though you were doing "Bumps-a-Daisy." Pull his sleeve around with your left hand as you straighten your legs.

7. Bend forward from the hips with a rocking motion and drop your right shoulder. Your right arm goes forward and down, guiding his body. All movements in this step must be simultaneous. Pull up on your partner's sleeve with your left hand to help him take the fall in the proper position.

50. SCARF CHOKE OR
GARROTE THROW

This move is to be practiced by students only under an instructor's supervision and after they have gained proficiency in throwing and falling.

attack:

Your assailant attacks you from the rear with a scarf, a rope, or something similar. A lady's nylon stocking is often used for this purpose. He may be holding his hands at either side of your neck or he may cross his wrists.

escape and throw:

1. It is important in this move that you do not move your neck; any pulling motion will tighten the choke. With your feet planted and knees slightly bent, move your hips to the left and strike his solar-plexus with your right elbow as described in Counterblows (Atewaza). Right fist in your left hand; both wrists straight.

2. Drive your right elbow straight back—hard.

3. Slip your right arm around his waist under his left arm. Grasp his right sleeve with your left hand. Bend your knees outward, straighten your back, and tuck in your chin. The position is the same as that in the previous move. Hold him close to your body with your right hand.

4. Throw with the Basic Hip Throw (Ogoshi). Push your hips back and up, pull his sleeve around with your left hand, straighten your legs, bend forward from the hips, and drop your right shoulder. Guide his body down with your extended right hand. Throughout the move keep the neck immobile. Let the hips do the moving.

This is an extremely hard fall even for an experienced Judo player, because the person being thrown has only the scarf to hang on to, and since the scarf slides over his partner's head it provides no support.

143

All of the moves you have been learning are basic techniques which can be adapted to different types of attack. It is impossible to determine what the exact reaction of the attacker to your counterattack will be. If he moves away from the counter you are applying, he will probably move into position for another type of counterattack. For example, a rear Wrist Lock can be changed to an Arm Lock without loosening your hold. You may use parts of one escape with different locks or counterblows. Stay loose and relaxed but alert for changes in his position.

In the event of a real attack, break his wrist or arm with a snapping, jerky motion as soon as the lock is applied. Do not hesitate—he must be incapacitated at the earliest opportunity and rendered harmless. Remember, it is your *life* you are protecting. If, feeling sorry for him, you hurt him only a little, he will in anger, redouble his efforts to harm you. By putting him out of commission you might be saving him from sentence to the electric chair for your murder; a broken arm or wrist will mend in a short time.

SPORT JUDO FOR WOMEN

The methods Professor Kano first formulated are ways of attack and defense based on the all-pervading principle of making the most efficient use of mental as well as physical energy and directing them to the accomplishment of a certain definite purpose. Then he applied this principle to the improvement of health, or physical education. From this, Judo has evolved into a sport.

There are two basic forms of training in Kodokan Judo: Kata, or form, and Randori, or free play. The Judo student is first taught simple throws in Kata. When the student has acquired proficiency in falling and throwing, she then practices the same moves in Randori. In Randori, you must accept with good grace your partner's throw. If your partner's technique does not upset your balance, you move away or throw your partner with a counter-throw. But if her technique is good, you take the throw without resistance. Randori is meant to be practice in technique, not contest.

The techniques of Judo, and its beauty, are best demonstrated in the Formal Katas. In the Formal Katas the moves are done in a prearranged sequence and manner. The one playing the part of the assailant is called Uke, or receiver. Excepting Katame-no-Kata and Seiryoku-zen'yô Kokumin Taiiku-no-Kata, each move of the Kata starts with Uke attacking his partner, Tori (or thrower) in a prescribed manner. Tori counters the attack also in a prearranged fashion. Every move of Uke and Tori in the Kata is predetermined.

The Formal Katas of the Kodokan

1. Nage no Kata — Forms of Throwing
2. Katame no Kata — Forms of Grappling
3. Kime no Kata — Forms of Decision
4. Juno Kata — Forms of Gentleness
5. Koshiki no Kata — Forms Antique
6. Itsutsu no Kata — Forms of Five
7. Goshiho no Kata — Forms of Self-Defense for Women
8. Goshinjitsu no Kata — Forms of Self-Defense for Men
9. Seiryoku-zen'yô Kokumin Taiiku no Kata — Forms of National Physical Education, Based on the Principle of Maximum Efficiency

Contest Judo, or Shiai, is competition between two male opponents. The match is conducted by a referee and two judges. Each competitor tries to throw the other without being thrown himself. The first to score one point (Ippon) by throwing the other cleanly, with good technique in the opinion of the referee, wins the match. A match may also be won by accumulating two half-points (Waza ari). A half-point is given to a throw that is almost perfect. A match may also be won by holding the opponent on the mat in a prescribed position for thirty seconds or by making the opponent concede the match with an Elbow Lock or a Judo Choke. In the event that no throws or points are scored, the referee and two judges award the match to the competitor with the better technique. These are the rules used in competition and championships. The first World Championship of Judo was held in Tokyo in May, 1956. Judo was first included in the Olympics in 1964.

The Kodokan sets the rules and precedents of Judo throughout the world. They have always maintained that women should not be allowed to compete in Shiai (contest Judo). In an effort to provide competition for women within the rules of the Kodokan, a form of Kata Competition has been developed. In Kata Competition, women perform the Formal Katas of Kodokan Judo and are scored on a points basis by a panel of three judges. This type of competition has been held in several different sections of the United States in the last two years. The Women's AAU Open Invitational Judo Kata Championships were held in New York in 1964 and 1965. These competitions serve to develop women's Judo by giving all women Judo students something to work for.

Besides official competitions, there are Randori Clinics (instruction lectures, demonstrations, and practices in which women can compete informally), and informal Randori, or free play, is also part of the training given by most Judo clubs.

A WORD TO THE WISE

Keep in mind that Judo is not infallible. It is only as good as the person applying it. The safest course is to avoid, whenever possible, situations which may be dangerous. For example, no intelligent girl will ever accept a ride with a strange man. But occasionally you might find yourself alone with a man you have just met. You may have met through mutual friends or at a party. What starts out as a group in the car may end up with just the two of you when the others have been driven home. Play it smart. Keep the conversation on general matters, sit fairly close to the door, and do not stop to park in a lonely section. If you should have a problem with your escort, be polite but firm. Talk your way out of it, if possible. Most men will respect your wishes and you, if they are sure you mean what you say. If it is necessary you can apply a Wrist Lock as in the Come-Along (Move 40). If you smoke, a cigarette can be an effective weapon, or a cigarette lighter well applied can discourage a potential attacker. If you are fighting for your life, anything goes. Even when you know your companion very well, avoid "Lovers' Lanes." The danger here may very well be not from him but from those who prey on lonely spots such as these. A more brightly lit area may not be as romantic but it will be much safer.

Whenever you are in a car, keep the doors locked, whether you are alone or with others. If you must stop to ask directions, open the windows only one or two inches. If anyone attempts to get into the car, step on the gas and drive away. Of course, never pick up hitchhikers.

Keep your parked car locked. When you approach it, have your keys in your hand ready to unlock the car without delay. When you get into the car, check the back seat to make sure no one is hiding there. If you drive into a dark, private garage, use your headlights to make sure the garage is empty before you unlock your car door.

When walking alone, try to avoid dark streets. If it is necessary to use these streets, walk as far away from the buildings as possible. Do not walk close to parked cars. If the traffic is light, walk in the street. When you pass a streetlight, watch your shadow. If someone is coming close to you, you will see his shadow. A cigarette is a useful weapon against a surprise attack. A mugger whose arm is suddenly thrust around your neck will remove his arm just as quickly if his hand is burned with a cigarette.

If you usually arrive home late at night in a dark area, it may be wise to take a taxicab. If you take a bus, try to have someone meet you at the bus stop. If no one can meet you, it is a good idea to stagger the time of your arrival so that you do not always take the same bus. If your family is waiting at home, let them know when you expect to arrive. The wisest procedure in this case is to call home when you are starting your trip. Then they will know when to expect you.

Never carry large sums of money. If an armed man demands your purse, give it to him. You can always replace its contents. Do not try to be a heroine. Discretion *is* the better part of valor.

It is a good idea to have your house or apartment key ready so that you will not have to stop on your doorstep to search for it. If you notice a strange man loitering in your apartment-house lobby, avoid him if possible. Notify the superintendent of his presence as soon as you can. When you enter an automatic elevator, close the door immediately. If another person follows you in, stand with your back against the wall close to the control panel. If a strange man enters, place your hand near the alarm button on the panel, ready for instant use. If he seizes you, use the escape or counter most applicable. You cannot run away from an attack made in an elevator until the door opens, so it is better to control the man with a lock or to use a take-down or a throw. In a takedown or a throw, the small confines of an elevator can work to your advantage. The man will hit the wall as well as the floor.

Women are often advised to scream. I feel a scream might cause an unstable assailant to panic. What is intended as a robbery can easily turn into an assault or a homicide. The attacker's first reaction is to try to silence you. The best course of action is to scream only if these three conditions are met: the man is unarmed, there is a distance of at least ten feet between you and him; there are people within earshot who will help you. Of course, as soon as you escape from his grip, run. Then you can scream your head off. If there is a police call box near, take the receiver off and ask for help. Knock on any door and ask for help, but do not enter a strange house. Stop a passing car—but do not get into the car, or you might find yourself in trouble again.

Keep your windows and doors locked when you are out of the house even for a minute. Many women in apartments have gone out to dispose of the garbage and returned to find an attacker in their room. Do not open the door to strangers. Every door should have a chain lock in constant use. A favorite gimmick used by thieves and rapists to gain admittance is to pretend they have come to deliver something. If this should happen when you are alone, tell the man to leave the delivery with the superintendent, or at the apartment next door if there are men there. If you come home and hear or see someone inside your apartment or house, do not enter. Go to the superintendent or to a neighbor and ask him to call the police. If you live alone, it might be a good idea to set up an alarm system of some sort with your neighbor. Most thieves or rapists are hesitant to enter an apartment or house that is guarded by a dog. A dog will warn you of intruders as well as protect you from them. Keep your shades or curtains drawn at night. Prospective attackers will not know whether you are alone if they cannot see you.

At night in subways try to stay with the crowd. When the subways are nearly empty, move to the car with the most people. When you leave the subway, stay with the other passengers when possible until you leave the station. Do not walk alone down long passageways. It is better to go up to the street at the main exit. If you are assaulted in an empty subway car by a man standing in front of you, turn sideways and kick at his closest knee. If you are standing, use the bars or straps for support as you kick. If you are sitting down, turn sideways in your seat before kicking.

According to the New York Transit Authority, the incidence of felonies in the New York City subways increased by 52 percent during 1964. There were 1,707 reported felonies committed in these subways. The FBI's crime reporting system has revealed that in the same period 173,406 major crimes were committed in New York City. Is there any doubt about why I feel so strongly that all women should learn to protect themselves? But most of all, use your good common sense to stay out of trouble.